PREPARATION BREEDS SUCCESS

PREPARATION BREEDS SUCCESS

Technical Sales of Customized, Capital, and Engineered Products

Michael F. Hotchkiss

ARCHWAY PUBLISHING

Archway Publishing books may be ordered through booksellers or by contacting:

Archway Publishing
1663 Liberty Drive
Bloomington, IN 47403
www.archwaypublishing.com
1-(888)-242-5904

Because of the dynamic nature of the Internet, any web addresses or links contained in this book may have changed since publication and may no longer be valid. The views expressed in this work are solely those of the author and do not necessarily reflect the views of the publisher, and the publisher hereby disclaims any responsibility for them.

Any people depicted in stock imagery provided by Thinkstock are models, and such images are being used for illustrative purposes only. Certain stock imagery © Thinkstock.

ISBN: 978-1-4808-0772-3 (sc)
ISBN: 978-1-4808-0773-0 (hc)
ISBN: 978-1-4808-0774-7 (e)

Library of Congress Control Number: 2014910253

Printed in the United States of America

Archway Publishing rev. date: 7/08/2014

To my dear, departed father, Thomas Welch Hotchkiss. A brilliant engineer for his entire career; company founder; loving, devoted husband; and, simply, a great dad. While he did not teach me how to sell, he taught me, by example, how to treat people. Same thing.

CONTENTS

Introduction xi

Chapter 1   Know Why Your Customers Buy 1

Chapter 2   Get to Know Your Customer 5

Chapter 3   Information Gathering 14

Chapter 4   The First Meeting with a Potential Customer 19

Chapter 5   Getting in the Door 23

Chapter 6   Filling the Customer's Need 28

Chapter 7   Be Honest about Your Capabilities 30

Chapter 8   Communication Is King 33

Chapter 9   Dealing with Price or Delivery Resistance 36

Chapter 10   The Real Voice of the Customer 40

Chapter 11   Closing the Deal 44

Chapter 12   When to Say No 47

Chapter 13   Treating Customers Right 51

Chapter 14   Earning Your Customer's Confidence 55

Chapter 15   Establishing Rapport 58

Chapter 16   Do What You Commit to Do 62

Chapter 17   Never Make Excuses 65

Chapter 18   Dealing with Problems 68

Chapter 19   Handling Angry Customers 72

Chapter 20   Handling Comparisons to Competitors 75

Chapter 21   Post-order Issues 81

Chapter 22   Dealing with Your Inner Circle 84

Chapter 23   Selling through Field Sales and Inside Sales 88

Chapter 24   Selling through Agents and Distributors 90

Chapter 25   Marketing Industrial and Capital Products 95

Chapter 26   Other Product Promotion Techniques 111

Chapter 27   Public Speaking 116

Chapter 28   Closing Thoughts 119

About the Author 121

Failing to prepare is preparing to fail.
—John Wooden

INTRODUCTION

I have spent the better part of my twenty-five-year career selling capital equipment and technically engineered industrial products. These products were, in most cases, specific to a desired task—hence involved customer interaction and detailed discussion to formulate a potential solution. Every selling transaction I have been involved with has been unique. Ranging from $15 million petrochemical projects to $1,000 hydraulic pumps, every customized product sale had its own identity, and they required dealing with different personalities and strategies to completely understand the chance of success. While there are many similarities among various selling opportunities, I believe every sale is a unique entity, each one requiring different tactics. While this is particularly important with capital or industrial products, the same tactics can be applied to selling cell phones or vacuum cleaners.

The main intention of this book is to focus on selling capital and industrial goods. As such, there is not much material devoted to strategies or advice for the door-to-door salesperson or telemarketer (only one of the sales techniques that now include spam e-mails and targeted pop-up ads based on what you search for on engineered and company websites). Selling commodity products is different from selling capital and engineered products. Shotgun marketing—that is a team of folks making phone calls or sending automated e-mails—does not apply when selling capital and industrial products. While many of the topics

I present here are geared toward selling non-commodity items, many of the points can be applied to selling any products in any sales situation, as long as you are willing to prepare and do your homework. I am not a big fan of the blind selling process, regardless of the product.

I had the privilege of having my first job with Farrel Corporation, a producer of large plastic and rubber processing machinery. The company was loaded with really smart people yet was small enough that I had access to all their brainpower. Because the company was small, I also had the chance to learn about everything—engineering design, applications, project management, process control, polymer technology, and, most importantly, technical marketing and selling. I must say a huge thank-you to my first boss, Doug Mosher, for allowing all of this to happen. While an engineer to the core, Doug recognized and understood the individuals he was responsible for and, in my case, enabled me to go in the direction that was preordained for me: to be in project management and technical sales.

As time and technology move along, doing customer homework has become increasingly simple. Beyond the straightforward Google (or any other search engine's) approach, company websites are valuable sources of information, as are blogs and social media. There is also nothing wrong with engaging in phone conversations with a potential client and asking company-specific questions, and even personal ones, to prepare for your impending face-to-face conversation.

You will also see that I repeat some suggestions in different chapters. This is to reinforce that nobody likes unexpected surprises, especially when it's something he or she could have found with a little digging. This would include information about a company, such as how long it has been in business, how it was incorporated, and what principal markets it serves, to name a few. The same goes for the person or people you may engage with. While not all of this information may be readily available, it is worth the time to try to find out what you can in advance. If some things are not obtainable, then explore those issues during first contact. Don't just start with what your company's capabilities and products are all about. A general question about the weather can open the door to a more comfortable exchange. The most important aspects of the technical selling process, and how they are applied to similar yet different situations by making the dialogue relaxed, are:

- to know ahead of time what you are dealing with;
- to create a strategy to deal with what you discover; and
- to store what you would like to discover in your memory bank or notebook.

As pointed out to me in the early stages of my selling career, the sales profession is the only widespread occupation that is not taught in any institute of higher learning as a degreed program. It is hard to understand why or how a noted business school does not have a major in sales. A plethora of training courses are available to up-and-coming sales and marketing professionals. Dale Carnegie comes to mind. However, as the main theme of this book emphasizes, sales is not a process you can read about in a book (except this one, of course) or prepare for in the same way for all situations. Selling and marketing retail products, financial services, used cars,, lawn-care products, or widgets all require a different mind-set. While your sales message can be beaten into someone with canned speeches, never giving up or saying no, applying pressure, or bombarding a target with phone calls, mailings, or e-mails are techniques that do not apply to every situation. The difference between technical sales and selling consumer products (or *sell-a-vision*) is like the difference between a pollywog and an elephant: completely different animals.

Selling engineered and technical goods that may have different purposes, uses, and features to achieve what the customer needs is far more complicated than selling Hula-Hoops. Hopefully, the thoughts and real-life experiences presented in the following pages will provide some insight into the complexity of selling technical goods and give you some solid suggestions for doing so effectively.

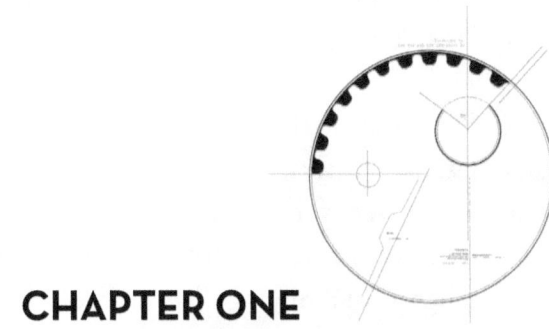

CHAPTER ONE

Know Why Your Customers Buy

I was taught by one of my early mentors, Al Shaio at Farrel Corporation that "nobody buys from someone they don't like." While this is usually true, it is not 100 percent accurate. There are forces in place in corporations that you may be unaware of that drive buying decisions, and those forces may have nothing to do with being pals with the buying agent with whom you are dealing. One example of these unknown forces is your new friend's boss or a purchasing manager who is looking to flex some muscle over suppliers—perhaps to save money, to meet a goal, to make him or herself look good to the boss, or just because he has a large ego. (More later on egos.) It, unfortunately, could also be a more senior manager who has a history with a competitive supplier, which could be from a long-standing relationship or might be linked to some ulterior motive. (Yes, corruption still exists.) It is very important to learn this in advance if you can, by tapping into resources that may be familiar with the nuances of the company or the individual you are working with. Most times the best approach to selling is not to regurgitate your spiel but to ask questions and become more informed about the customer and the company. The buyer/seller relationship can also be impeded (or helped)

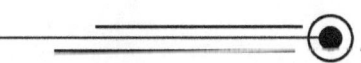

by the attitude of the ultimate decision maker. Some purchasing agents or buyers feel it is their given right to treat sellers poorly. It is important to find this out prior to engaging with a customer or to be astute enough to learn this during initial contacts. The ultimate buying person may be trained just like an average salesperson in reverse order—that is, getting the most while paying the least, rather than getting less while paying the most. Both thoughts are distasteful but are a reality in some cases, so be conscientious when analyzing what you are facing.

Learn before Engaging

As a rule, I have found that most customers I have engaged with are fair, ethical, and educated in their craft, but there are exceptions. To ignore this can cost your company business. Learn about these factors as related to your customer before engaging. If you can't do it in advance, then ask questions during the initial contact. Don't try to sell a product before you know as much as possible about the application, who you are dealing with, and the customer in general. This is especially important if you're dealing with different cultural or geographic situations within the United States or, more importantly, when dealing with customers in different countries.

For example, I handled many selling events in Asia while I was based in Singapore. In my experience, no quotation as written was ever accepted without discussion. This could include price negotiation, delivery, or contract terms. Time value was not even a factor. While you may be used to having a twenty-minute phone conversation with a customer in the United States to get an order, the same transaction in China may take days. If you are aware of this beforehand, the process will be much less frustrating, you will know to exercise patience, and it will be invaluable to your success at closing the deal.

Here's a True Story

I was in Tianjin, China, in the mid-nineties with a couple of work colleagues, negotiating a $3–4 million order. The potential buyer had us in one room and our competitor in another room down the hall. The buyer went back and forth, handing us slips of paper with the current offered price and asking if we could do better. When we countered, the buyer left with a new slip of paper to report the current "recommended" price to our competitor. We eventually gave notice that we were making our final offer and were prepared to leave without an order. Did I mention this was on December 23 with a twenty-four-hour travel time to get home? Do you think they didn't know that we wanted to get home in time for Christmas? Of course they did.

After these gyrations, the buyer said they wanted to accept our offer and finalize the contract. Another few hours of deliberations over the terms of the deal went by, and about one in the morning they were typing amendments to the contract (amazing, considering China was already manufacturing a vast amount of the world's PC components). Midway through these amendments, the typewriter ribbon broke and they did not have a spare ribbon. Christmas in the United States was now in serious question. The woman doing the typing raised an eyebrow, smiled, and reached into her purse to extract a sewing kit. She removed the broken ribbon from the '60s vintage typewriter and stitched it back together. Without a comment, she put the ribbon back and finalized the amendments. It was now after two in the morning, but we made it back to the United States just in time for Santa Claus, with our nice new order.

Every Sale Is Unique

To summarize, every sale is a unique entity. Thinking you can apply a single technique to sell a product to different customers is pure folly. No question is a bad question. I know that sounds trite, but remember that this is a critical aspect of the selling process. If the customer has a reason to ask something, no matter how inane it may seem, it is an opportunity for you to learn. You need to be more concerned if they don't ask any questions at all.

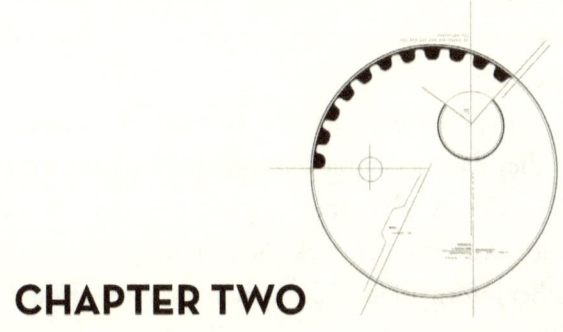

CHAPTER TWO

Get to Know Your Customer

A consistent theme throughout this book is: do your homework. This can be applied to all situations, from inquiry response, to quoting, to negotiations, to after-sales activities. So, get to know as much as possible about your customer, situation to be dealt with and your contact prior to any engagement, whether it is by phone, e-mail, or face-to-face. Gathering information is not difficult in today's world.

Research Your Potential Customer

Nobody likes unexpected surprises. Don't risk finding out something at the in-person meeting that you should have found out beforehand. This includes information about the company, such as how long they have been in business, how they were incorporated, and what principal markets they serve. The same goes for the person or people you may engage with at the company. While not all of this information may be readily available, it is worth the time to try finding out in advance. If it's not obtainable, then explore during your first in-person contact. Don't just start with what your company's capabilities and products

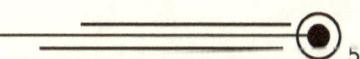

are all about. A general question about who won the game last night or some other innocuous comment can open the door to a more fruitful exchange.

Thoroughly peruse the potential customer's website. Check to see if they have social media pages or blogs and examine them completely. If you know of another supplier, colleague, or individual who has dealt with the customer, pick their brains about tendencies, culture, or any other information. One cautionary note: if you do not know the person who is offering insight too well, take anything said with a grain of salt until you verify it. Information is only valuable if it's verified and not subjective.

Also, learn as much as possible about the person you are contacting at the client company. This can be done through people who may have had contact with him or her, or it can be done subtly with a phone call or e-mail. When doing so, mention something personal about yourself, which can open the door to learning or asking something about the other person's interests, hobbies, family, and so on. This information can be invaluable with the initial ice breaking.

Know the Company's DNA

It's important to know the nature of the organization you are dealing with. In many cases, this is learned from multiple visits, not usually on an initial contact. Fortunately, the Internet enables us to learn more about an organization than previously possible. Use Google and other search engines. Homework has become easier with the advent of modern technology.

Although technology is a valuable tool, direct communication is still the most crucial part of the sales process. You can learn much by a few phone calls to resources who have had contact with or done business with your prospect. All of these options should be exploited before making initial contact with your potential customer.

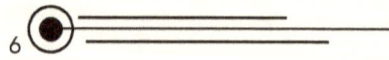

Cultural Considerations

Having had the privilege of selling in many different countries, I have become acutely aware of the importance of knowing the business practices and subtleties of the country in which I'm operating. In China for example, exchanging business cards is more than a flip across the table. One must extend his or her card with two hands and with a slight bow of the head and wait for the card to be accepted in the same manner. The person receiving the card will study it and acknowledge with gravity of the presenter's name and position in the company. Do the same in return when someone is presenting you with this valuable piece of paper. It is a sign of respect that is certainly unfamiliar to those of us in the United States.

One Thing You Shouldn't Do

Some time ago, I was with one of my field salesman at a new customer in Ohio. On our drive to the appointment, I asked what the salesman knew about the customer. His answer disappointed me: "I guess we'll find out when we get there." When we arrived, we were escorted to a conference room with about a dozen people, including engineers and purchasing and management staff. As an icebreaker, my colleague told a joke that, at the very least, could be considered colorful. Really, it was ribald. It turned out the company we were visiting was owned and run by the Amish, and they only employed other Amish. Needless to say, it was a very short visit.

Whether handling a prospect directly or overseeing the efforts of a sales staff, agent, or industrial distributors, it is best to get to know the entire organization you are dealing with. This is simpler if you have complete control and you are dealing with the person at your client company who is involved with the product you are selling. It is more complicated when dealing with an agent, and very tough when trying to get a distributor to gather the desired information. Using third parties to cover more ground can be valuable, but it requires more direct involvement and hand holding than dealing with an employee.

What Is the Customer's Hierarchy?

The level of difficulty in learning your prospect's tendencies depends on the effort your point of contact is willing to engage in and how much control you have over the process. If you are the point of contact, then all it requires is your motivation to learn about the customer. If you are supervising the person who is managing the sales process, you can play coach, offer instructions, or even issue an order about what is required. Typically, sales agents have their own interests in mind, as they most likely work on a commission basis. Bad agents do not want to put much effort into the sales process, but if you convince them of the potential results, they can be coerced. Distributors, on the other hand, are committed to provide results for their own company. If they see another opportunity with more likelihood of success, there is not much you can do to turn their focus to your task at hand. A distributor representative does not report to you. He or she already has a boss who dictates priorities. In my experience, it's not easy to get distributors to do an exploratory mission to learn about a prospect, unless there is a foreseeable and tangible benefit to the individual or to their company.

At Trade Shows
No Yes or No Questions

When talking to your potential customer, the best approach to selling is not to regurgitate your spiel, but to ask questions and become more informed about the customer and the company. One tried and true practice is to avoid asking yes or no questions, primarily to avoid that *no* response. If you ask a customer if they need something from you and they say no, you have nowhere to go from there. If they say yes, you might ask about specific options or ask another question that requires a response other than no. That can lead to a dialogue.

Have you ever been in a furniture store or used-car showroom and been approached by a salesperson who asked, "May I help you with anything?" Your answer probably was, "No, just looking," and the salesperson followed up with, "Well, please let me know when you need assistance." A missed opportunity, for sure. Even "What can I do for you today?" or a question about the contacts interests or role in their company is better than a question that begs a no answer.

No "How Can I Help You?"

I used to attend many major trade shows staffed with twenty-five or more salespeople from our company. My boss would gather everyone before the opening each day and ask what had transpired during the show thus far that might be of interest. We all shared any tidbits of information we'd gleaned from talking to show attendees, whether they were potential buyers, vendors, or the competition. He concluded each session with the statement, "If I hear anyone asking attendees at our booth 'Can I I help you? You're fired." While I always assumed this to be rhetorical, it got the message across. "How has the show been going for you so far?" or "Who do you work for and what do you do?" are preferable, as they are less likely to get the dreaded no response and a view of the person's back walking away. Be sure to give yourself options for starting a dialogue and not be automatically dismissed. At the same time, be savvy enough to recognize a window shopper who would prefer to browse. They're most likely not a hot prospect, so let them browse.

In one particular instance at show Chicago, I noticed two gentlemen hovering around a new machine we were launching with notepads and pencils. I approached them to ask about what their interests were in the machine. As they scurried away, I saw the name tags they were wearing and it was a competitor. Keep your eyes and ears open. You can learn much from perception without conversing.

A Case of My Company Being the Customer

I recently was seeking current price and availability of a particular component from a supplier so I could get a quote to a customer. I e-mailed the field salesperson responsible for our account, requesting a quote on a standard component they make and that we have purchased numerous times. Two days later, I got copied on an e-mail that field salesperson, my local rep, had sent to an inside salesperson at the home office. My rep asked the salesperson to handle the inquiry as he was "too busy" to deal with my request. If I'd had a choice to get the product from another supplier, I would have done so in a heartbeat. I'm sure you've had similar experiences.

By the way, this is a classic exception to the rule "do not buy from someone you don't like." I knew before I sent the request that I did not like this rep, but I had no other alternative, since the item was specified by the customer. Frankly, I was relieved to work with someone else to get the information I'd requested.

A Case in Point

Here's an example of a failure to collect accurate information about a potential customer. I receive frequent calls or e-mails from Search Engine Optimization (SEO) companies telling me our website does not appear on the first page of Google and other search engines. They are wrong. Our company has been using an ethical and respected SEO company for years, and our company's website ranks in the top three positions on Google, Bing, and other search engines for almost every key word we use. If these companies had actually checked, they could have taken a different tactic with me, like selling value rather than supposed low page ranking. Instead they got a hasty no thanks followed by a dial tone.

The more information you can gather about a customer, whether new or existing, the more successful you will be communicating effectively and ultimately selling your product or service.

Selling Dos and Don'ts
Do Ask Questions

First and foremost, when you meet with a potential customer, leave your ego in the parking lot. It is far more effective to gain trust and gather information by asking questions and learning as much as you can from your contact. Particularly with sales of technical equipment, it can be an immediate turnoff to initiate the conversation with what products you sell and how great they are. It is equally as bad or worse to start by talking about yourself. This is not unlike the telemarketing calls you may receive in the evening, when the callers don't let you say hello before they launch into their canned pitch. Work the discussion so you can find your client's needs, problems and issues, so you can become a solution solver and not the proverbial pitchman.

Do Let the Customer Be in Charge

It cannot be emphasized enough how keeping quiet and asking the occasional question is a far more effective way to determine a customer's needs. If you recognize an issue that you're an expert on, or your products may help solve, casually introduce the idea that there might be a relatively simple solution. But let the customer be in charge of the conversation. If you're asked about a certain product or an application, you can respond with confidence. However, do not overstate or boast about the capabilities of your product. Just as important, if you do not know the answer to a specific question about or application being discussed, "I don't know, but I will find out," is a far better response than faking it. Overconfidence and ego can be a huge deterrent to relationship building.

Do Take Time for a Friendly Chat

Once you have an established relationship with a customer, subsequent communications can start on a lighter note or with a personal inquiry, such as "How is/are the family/pet/parents?" Most people have limited time these days, so keep the chitchat to a minimum. But a friendly engagement with a personal reference unrelated to business can go a long way to gaining trust and establishing a personal relationship.

Don't Go Negative

Remember that starting any conversation with a negative can instantly put your customer to the defensive. If you are asked whether you or your company can perform a certain task, the last word you want to start your reply with is no. Rather, acknowledge the question and give a friendly explanation of why you may not be able to accommodate the request, instead of a "why the hell do you want that?" attitude. "That sounds like an interesting application. I hope you find a solution" and "Thank you for your interest" are always good ways to respond to an undoable request. Thank them for the consideration and express your hope to do business one day.

Don't Talk about Controversial Topics

Use discretion in your choice of words, comments, and opinions. In today's politically correct world, you have to assume the person you're talking to may be sensitive to particular issues, whether political, cultural, or religious. It is always possible to offend someone by something you say, so err on the side of not saying anything when it comes to emotionally charged topics.

Don't Excuse Bad Behavior

That said, there is no reason to allow potential customers to be offensive or rude without a response. The response should be handled carefully, but you can object to bad behavior. I learned a lesson when I was a sophomore salesman visiting one of our regional offices. The regional manager had set up appointments across the state with existing and potential customers with specific times and an agenda. It was a grueling schedule, yet well thought out and precisely timed. We arrived at one of our scheduled appointments on time, announced our presence to the receptionist (yes, there used to be a person called a receptionist), and were asked to sit down to wait for our contact. We sat there for about thirty minutes with no other contact. My colleague stood up and said, "Let's go." He dropped our business cards with the receptionist and said we had another appointment to get to. He did not make an excuse or complain about being treated with disrespect. As it turned out, our contact wasn't able to meet us at the scheduled time, gave no explanation why, yet later sent a significant amount of business our way. We like to think it was because we didn't burn our bridges with a rude response.

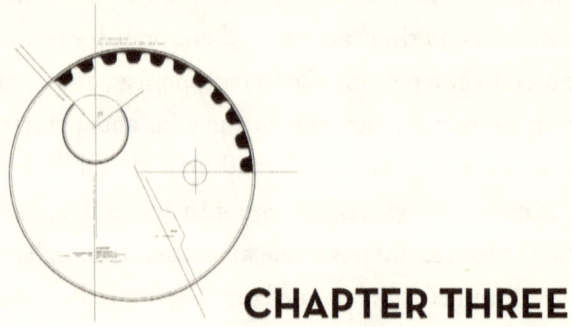

CHAPTER THREE

Information Gathering

Information gathering for an encounter with a customer or potential customer is situational. Every meeting will be different, and preparation for the topic(s) to be discussed will make you come across as someone who is prepared and knows what he or she is talking about. Far too many meetings are set up without a specific agenda. You may be asked to meet to talk about a new project or application. It is perfectly acceptable to ask for further details, including the topics, the other participants, and the overall objective of the discussions.

Setting an Agenda

If you are involved with scheduling and setting the agenda, then this is just a matter of asking the contact about the key items. If a colleague is the point person, be sure to express how proper preparation can only be achieved by getting details about the meeting. An outside sales representative, agent, or distributor may call and say, "The customer wants to see you next week and I think it would really help." This is a common practice. No disrespect to non-company sales services, but they also have other product lines and customers, and they may not feel they have the time to do the homework. There is nothing wrong with a phone call or an e-mail to your rep asking for specific information prior to the meeting. You may not get all your answers, but at least you will be smarter when you get there.

A list of things you would want to know prior to a meeting:

1. Who will be attending the meeting?

2. What is the pecking order of those involved?

3. What is the culture of the company—cheap, quality driven, time critical?

4. What are the details about the project or application relative to what you can offer?

5. Does the customer already have the same or a similar application in use?

6. If so, what current equipment is being used?

7. If they are using other equipment in the same application, why are they looking for an alternative? Are they dissatisfied in some way or are they just shopping?

"I'll Get Back to You on That"

The above list could go on and on, but those are the basics. It can be customized to the specific topics that need to be covered and the people involved. The important thing is to start thinking about what could arise and try to prepare for anything. If you do get blindsided by an issue, try to behave as if you anticipated the situation by remaining calm and not showing emotion. The answer "I'm not sure about that, but I will find out" is perfectly acceptable. In fact, it's favorable to "I'll need to check with my superiors." There is no faster way to lose a customer's confidence in you than to pass a decision or reply on to the powers that be. The customer will automatically want to deal with someone who has the authority or knowledge to answer all concerns. It is equally bad to fudge when you are unsure, as this will invariably come back to bite you later. It is a far greater display of confidence to tell customers you will get back to them than to fake an answer you are unsure of.

Other Sources of Information

If you cannot get all the answers from the customer, work colleagues, or sales reps, then get outside the box and try other methods to learn what you can. Sources of information can be other vendors who are not in direct competition with you but have a relationship with the prospect. Internet searches of company news, events, or announcements can also be revealing. There may even be news releases published in appropriate trade journals that shed some light on the company culture. Obviously, you would go through the company's website from first page to the last as part of the preparation process. If the company has a blog, read it. If it has a Facebook page, like it. If it has a Twitter account, follow it. If any of the players are on LinkedIn, see if you can learn something about them (although stay away from requesting becoming a contact until you actually get to know them).

First Impressions Are Important

While it may seem trivial, you can pick up tidbits when you arrive at the customer's location, especially upon a first encounter. What is the facility like? Is it well maintained? Is it old-school industrial? Are there picnic tables outside for employees (a sign of caring about the workers)? What does the reception area look like? If there is a receptionist, what is his or her appearance like? How are you greeted? An appropriately dressed and professional receptionist who greets with a smile says a lot about an organization. Are there plaques hanging, such as rewards, letters of appreciation, or notices of community service? Do they sponsor Little League or charity events? Is there a mission statement in plain view? All of these subtleties say something that you may be able to use during the ensuing discussions.

I recently visited a relatively new customer for the first time with our distributor that was covering the account. The distributor salesman had been dealing with the customer for years for a variety of fluid-power products and custom applications. Being a wily veteran of forty-plus years in selling fluid-power products, he had covered all the bases and given me a complete background on the customer—its tendencies, the competition, and the parties we would be meeting. About the only thing he did not mention was what their operation looked like, both inside and out. Since the customer was a machine tool integrator, albeit a prominent one, I was not expecting much beyond an industrial Butler-style building with a minimum amount of accoutrements. I was happily surprised to walk through a well-maintained parking lot to a nicely landscaped building, freshly painted. We were greeted in a clean, up-to-date, and tastefully furnished lobby by a professional receptionist, who smiled as she politely asked who we were there to see. While waiting for a contact to come collect us, I wandered the spacious lobby, replete with well-framed photographs of machines the company had built, as well as industry awards and recognition of membership in a host of industrial and community organizations.

This first impression made me feel comfortable and confident that we, along with our veteran distributor, could establish a solid and mutually beneficial business relationship.

With the tremendous growth of the Internet, your company's web footprint is most likely the first impression people will get of your organization. More details coming up on web presence and how important a tool the Internet can be. Nonetheless, it remains important to put on the most professional effort when customers visit. If you have the authority, ensure the reception area is at least clean, if not impressive.

Greet visitors personally and in a timely fashion. Be sure to offer your guests coffee or water on arrival. Depending on the agenda and the time required, organize snacks or a lunch. If you do not have a staff capable of setting up a nice spread, hire a catering service. Little things do count and do make a positive impression.

Some things that can have the opposite effect of a good first impression:

1. When the reception area is an unmanned room the size of a phone booth with a directory and a sign that instructs you to call your contact

2. When the aforementioned contact does not answer the phone, even after multiple attempts

3. When your host forgets you're coming

4. When your host(s) are disorganized and unprepared for the prearranged agenda

5. When the meeting room is not set up and your host scrambles to find chairs or other equipment and materials that could have had been arranged for long before the meeting

6. When you are not offered a refreshment upon arrival

7. When you receive uncordial treatment before, during, and after the meeting

8. When the customer is distracted and not engaged—signs of this include texting or taking phone calls during a meeting

Remember to be friendly and receptive. Be prepared and engaged at all times. It really pays off to do the simple things.

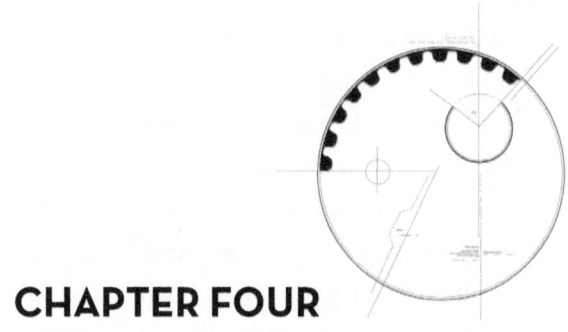

CHAPTER FOUR

The First Meeting with a Potential Customer

Preparation is more than learning all you can about a potential customer or putting your presentation together for a speaking engagement. It is critical to be ready for each customer interaction, whether it is a phone call, face-to-face encounter, or a larger meeting with many people. Find out what the meeting is about and what objectives the customer may have. Strategize how you will address this agenda while getting a positive message across. If you can, get to know as much as possible about the person or people you will be meeting or addressing. If you can find out personal information, such as outside interests or family life, use this to your advantage to create trust and friendliness during your initial encounter. Casually introduce what you already know about the customer, such as culture or personal interests.

A critical part of sales strategy is understanding, in advance, the customer's requirements. Are they overly cost conscientious? Do they have specific vendor requirements, such as ISO, QS-9000, or another quality certification? Are you aware of any competitors? If so, what are their strengths and weaknesses? Is delivery an issue? What is the hierarchy of the company? Are you actually speaking with a decision maker, a decision influencer, or someone who passes information up the ladder with little final say-so? Ask questions once you get there if you don't know this kind of information in advance. Most people like to be asked about themselves, what they do, or who they work for. Use that to your advantage.

Find out what your prospect looks for in a company. Is it financial stability? Perhaps history or longevity in the business is important. Do they require certain quality control certificates or have other preferences in a supplier? Do they want to know the structure of the organization? This goes back to being observant, opening your ears, and asking questions. It is surprising what makes people or organizations operate and what they look for in their partners.

You probably won't be able to collect and ascertain all this information prior to a first meeting, but these are points to consider as part of your preparation. It is immensely helpful to do this sort of background check on your customer's company and structure. There is a plethora of resources for you to go to get information. It is worth taking the time to tap into every resource available to learn as much as you can. It likely can make the difference between your success and failure.

Find Out the Purpose of the Meeting

Another strategy is establishing contact prior to the first meeting and learning all things possible about the upcoming appointment. Is this a getting-to-know-you meeting or is there another purpose? Knowing the agenda of the person or persons you are meeting with can completely change your preparation tactics. For example, if you find out the focus is to look for an alternative to something they already have purchased, you may choose a more aggressive tactic. This is more likely the case if they initiate contact. If the customer is responding to a plea from you via e-mail or phone call, then more caution and silence is prudent. In that case, your goal is to learn why they even decided to reply. Very few people respond positively to an unsolicited contact. When they do, there is a reason, so tread lightly.

Demonstrate Sincere Interest

On your initial visit to a customer, after having broken the ice with some personal snippet, demonstrate sincere interest in the company. Most people are proud of what they do and where they work. Asking to see the facilities and learn more about the operation goes a long way to building trust. (This truly should be sincere, and by nature, any decent salesperson has this natural trait of curiosity.) Who doesn't enjoy showing off what they do and what their role may be in their place of business? If this approach is met with disdain, then you are talking to the wrong person.

Preparation and Patience Paid Off

I was engaged with a project in the late nineties selling equipment to the world's first nylon-recycling plant. I enlisted our inside sales crew to help put the proposal together and be part of the entire process. The potential customer paid numerous visits to our lab to simulate the process, which had not been done before. Based on all the tests, and coupled with numerous specification changes, we modified quotations and the scope of supply over the course of more than a year. Our company, including the inside staff, worked tirelessly to handle all the changes associated with the $6 million project for a new processing technology.

After all these gyrations, we were invited to the client's headquarters in Atlanta for a "discussion." I surmised this was a key word for negotiation, as we had finally found a system that met their requirements. It didn't hurt that I had developed a good relationship with the project manager and was able to speak candidly to him about what to expect at the meeting. I prepped my team and booked the trip with mild trepidation. Our first meeting included our customer's lead purchasing agent, along with all of their technical staff that was associated with the process. Our team of technical salespeople and the production processing staff sat nervously across the table from them. After we'd exchanged pleasantries, the first person to speak was the purchasing agent-in-charge. I will never forget my surprise at what came from the mouth of this purchasing professional. He said, "You have done a ton of work to help us get this process to where our technical people feel comfortable. Because of that, we are not going to negotiate the quoted price." In all my years of selling capital machinery, I had never heard these words, and I could hardly contain my giddiness as I knew I had about a 5 percent cushion to negotiate. After a few changes in the terms and an agreed-upon delivery improvement, we had a deal.

One of the highlights of my career selling capital equipment was getting on the elevator with that team of people who had made it possible and hearing one of our young engineers—only about three years out of engineering school, and who had busted his butt during the process— let out a primal scream of satisfaction. He'd earned it, because he had prepared and strategized every step of the way. It made me very proud. It was worth every ounce of our effort to hear that response of satisfaction.

Once you know what your customers need, you can gain their confidence based on the merits of your product and your level of commitment to support them and be responsive.

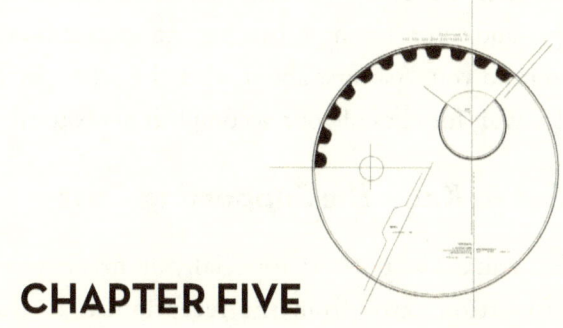

CHAPTER FIVE

Getting in the Door

In today's world, schmoozing customers is mostly extinct. Whereas taking a client to lunch or out for a few drinks after work used to be commonplace, it is rarely acceptable now, nor even an expected tactic. So, how do you get your prospect's attention enough to like you, or at least to engage in a discussion? There is no one answer, and that's the problem with many sales training programs that use the same strategy regardless of who you are dealing with or what the potential customer really needs.

It's Like a First Date

Think of your initial contact as a first date. Begin with small talk and show interest in what your potential customer does. Get to know the client's interests, whether personal or related to business. Work your way up to displaying an understanding of what the business is about and what they are looking for. Once engaged (no pun intended), and when you have determined that there is a potential fit, slowly integrate your products or services in a positive way. Do not push, but show enthusiasm about the potential to become partners to help improve both of your positions and companies. No first date wants to hear a monologue about you and your accomplishments, no matter how impressive they may seem to you. Ask first about what the other person enjoys and likes to do. Wait for tales of your accomplishments until you are asked.

Get to Know the Supporting Cast

It is equally important, especially on first contact, to get to know the supporting cast—from the receptionist, to the managers working with your contact, to those in charge of the operation. You will be surprised how helpful this will be for engaging in future visits. Walking in the door to a facility and saying, "Hello, Fran, I'm back to see John again" will most likely elicit a smile and prompt action to track down John.

Assuming you have done the appropriate pre-meeting research, try to remember the names of those who work with John or might become part of the discussion. Engage everyone personally with eye contact and a smile, without being phony. Ask about their backgrounds, their roles in the company, and even their families and outside interests. "What do you do in your spare time?" is a perfectly good way to get to know who you are dealing with. People are more likely to engage in a discussion if you show interest in what is important to them inside and outside of the workplace.

Ask to Meet the Person Who Signs the Purchase Order

In many cases, the people you deal with in capital goods, technical, or industrial sales are not the ones who sign the purchase orders. There is no harm in asking about the person who will issue the PO. You can subsequently ask to meet the person so the order becomes more personal. Purchasing agents or buyers often think of those they are issuing orders to as vendors, in a generic sense. This can be softened if they have a name and personality they can recall when they place an order or attempt to negotiate. You do not have to be phoney or suck up. Just get to know the person signing the order as part of the process. The more you can engage the organization, the better your chance for success.

Know the Company's Hierarchy

It's as important to know the company's hierarchy. In most cases, people down the chain from the decision maker have influence on the decision, including the contact you are dealing with. Find out who reports to whom and what role they play; it can make a difference in securing a deal. Even better, get an introduction to all involved in the process, including the decision maker. Again, use personal contact to your advantage. Be more interested in them rather than spouting off about how much you can help them. This will yield greater success, and you will gain a better understanding of the prospect you are dealing with.

You cannot beg for an audience, but you can be persuasive as to how such an encounter could be of mutual benefit. You also should suggest to work within the other person's time frame and lay out, in detail, the objective(s) of the meeting. This can take five minutes or thirty minutes, or whatever the customer feels is appropriate. If you still hit the wall of silence, it's okay to accept that. Try to keep the door open for future interactions. You can say, "I understand you are too busy now to look at alternatives, but may I check back with you in three to six months?" If the rejection is blunt, then move on and chalk it up to one of the many negative reactions you will incur while prospecting.

Generally, being inquisitive and observant are the best ways to learn about a potential opportunity, even if it is down the road. Bank this information, if you think it is relevant, for future contact. Also, know that companies' goals and personnel are constantly shifting, so an initial negative reaction may change later.

Keep Track of Change

Companies are living and breathing organisms. Change occurs constantly, including management turnover as well as new hires, promotions, or layoffs, which can change the dynamic of a potential prospect. Keep track of who you have contacted and when and any notes you garnered. Go back periodically to this archive of rejection and consider giving it another try. Create your own code for what probability you may have of getting through, based on what the customer requires. Taking notes about all your conversations is an essential part of the process for future success.

Another True Story: I Never Saw It Coming ...

I was involved in a situation that I never saw coming. It was not only a business experience, but one for the pages of my life.

I had been living in Singapore for about four years and had traveled extensively across Asia. Now, being a pro at doing business in the region, I might have slacked off a bit on my homework mantra. I was invited by our Indonesian agent to a meeting with a developer who was working on a $600 million petrochemical plant to produce plastic. I had the sense to be skeptical, but could not resist a fact-finding meeting.

Our meeting was with the principal of the new venture, who had already secured a $600 million line of credit from the Indonesian government to start the project. The line of credit allowed him access to any or all of the funds as he desired. This was encouraging, as financing projects of that size often get mired in the investment/funding process.

So, we met this guy at an enormous office in an exclusive new office building in Jakarta. Once we were seated, he entered with a translator to start our initial discussions. I knew there was something amiss from the get-go, but I was already there.

He proceeded to explain the plan for the new plant and that a critical part would be the processing machinery, which my company offered. Prior to the meeting, we had sent a ballpark quotation for the equipment of around $15 million, a small but not insignificant part of the project.

After some discussion about the long-term plan and timing of the project, we were served tea. We then learned of the real purpose of the meeting. The principal of the project asked us through his translator for a favor. (By now, I had surmised this guy probably spoke perfect English.) He requested that my company donate $500,000 to help him build a hospital in his hometown in mainland China. It followed that we would gain favorable consideration for the order and would also get a wing of this new hospital named for our company.

After picking my jaw up off the floor, I whispered in our agent's ear that not only would our company be guilty of a crime under US law, but I would also be criminally liable for unethical business behavior if we even fathomed meeting this request. The meeting didn't last long after that.

About two weeks later, a huge story emerged that the guy behind the project had fled the country with his $600 million in cash. He was eventually found in China, extradited back to Jakarta, and wound up in jail. They never found the money. He was allowed to visit his family at home on certain weekends, under supervision. On one such visit, the supervising guard was either not paying attention or was well compensated for turning a blind eye. The man and his family disappeared, never to be found.

The story went international, including a front-page piece in the *Wall Street Journal*. The plant never got built. I often wonder why someone would ask for a $500,000 bribe if they were going steal $600 million the next week.

I was totally blindsided by this occurrence, but was not sure what I could have done in advance. Still, I had not pressed our agent for more details about this individual, his company, or the conditions of the financing before we met with him. Lesson learned.

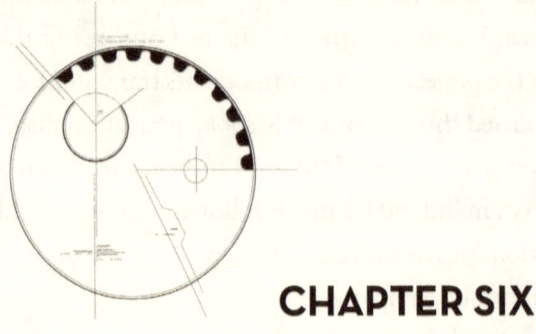

CHAPTER SIX

Filling the Customer's Need

A consistent theme throughout this book is homework. I cannot emphasize preparation too much, especially when it comes to technical sales. Whether capital or industrial equipment, these potential transactions require discussion and technical knowledge. Another mentor of mine instilled in me something that has been used in most sales-training seminars and courses: "If your customer wants a drill, sell the hole." This is actually very good advice for any salesperson. Promote the end result and work backward toward how your product can help achieve this result. The only way you can accomplish this and be convincing is to know the customer's desired requirement. Sell the hole.

Fill the Hole

Once you have convinced your customer you have an understanding of the hole they want to drill, you can offer a solution. Ask yourself, how big the hole is, how many do they need, and how frequently do they need them. When these questions are answered, you will be more educated and more prepared to offer a solution. But don't offer one if you really don't have a solution. Sometimes the best answer is, "Sorry, we do not have an answer for that application." You can add credibility by referring the customer to another resource that may help. But in order to make a referral, you should know what else is available. Homework again. This is counter to most salespeople's instincts, but may serve you better for future applications. If you can help a customer while forgoing a sale, you still gain credibility.

Taking this one step further, it is best to know what your potential customer has in mind or what the product or brand they currently use. If you can find this out, research the company and the product being used. Without takings shots at the competition, you can use this information to your advantage when making comparisons to what you have to offer. There's no need to make negative comments about the product your prospect is using. Just provide a compare and contrast description, which is far more acceptable than a repudiation of your competitor's product. This does require research (there's that homework again) in order to make the best promotion.

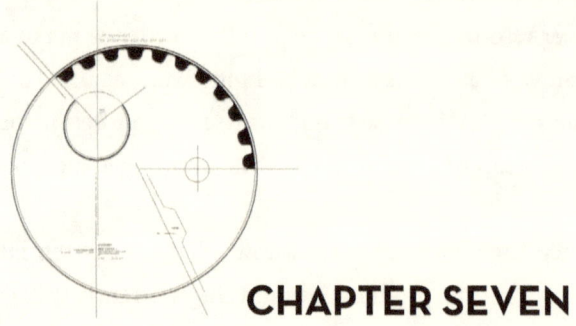

CHAPTER SEVEN

Be Honest about Your Capabilities

One of the worst mistakes sales professionals make is trying to offer too much or exaggerating their company's capabilities. It is understandable that you want to please people and offer something they need, but it's more important to recognize when you or your company cannot meet a requirement. I have never met or supervised a salesperson who likes to say, "Sorry, I cannot help you." That, however, is the best answer in some cases. A more friendly reply would be, "I appreciate your predicament, and we would love to help, but we do not have a resolution for your problem. I'll check if we have an alternative and get back to you."

Find Out What the Customer Needs

To determine the scope of the opportunity, first discover the customer's predicament or issue. Next, learn as much as possible about the extent and immediacy of their needs. Before offering any concrete solutions, talk with other people in your company about potential solutions and timing. Be sure to get everyone at your company who will be involved on the same page. Trying to do so after the fact is a far more difficult task. By nature, people are more apt to criticize or find a flaw once a deal is struck if they were not in the loop from the beginning. This is particularly true of those above your pay grade. Hindsight is easier to see and understand than foresight.

Don't Promise Something You Can't Deliver

Do not offer something if you're unsure it can be delivered. It is astonishing to me how frequently this occurs. This relates back to my point of getting everyone involved before offering anything, including but not limited to price, delivery, terms, or concessions that might be considered in order to make a deal. There is no better way to lose the trust and confidence of your customer than to not deliver on what was promised, even if it is out of your control.

Keep Everyone in Your Company in the Loop

As the sales director for my former company, I was involved with the development of a new product. The people involved in the project were all in tune with the program and, after about a year of effort, everyone agreed on a design. Or so I thought. From a sales and marketing perspective, we had a target price, along with sales materials and detailed technical specifications to assist with bringing the new machine to market. We also knew that the first sale was going to be a challenge because most companies do not like to buy serial number one. These machines would be built to order, as it was far too great an investment to build a prototype and test it. We had to rely on our past knowledge and the skill of the engineers, machinists, purchasing department, and assembly personnel to be able to produce the final product for the first time.

A Painful True Story

I went to visit a valuable customer in Mississippi with one of my field salespeople. This customer had many of our other machines and was a prime candidate for the new model. We had done our homework and sent the customer a quotation with a detailed specification before our visit. We were up front about the fact that we had yet to actually build one, but we also explained all the effort that had gone into the development. After reviewing all the materials we had prepared, they had some reservation about buying serial number one. A negotiation ensued, as we wanted to get that first sale. We made some price concessions that were more than usual for our other proven products, and we were elated when we left with an order.

Upon returning, we had our customary enter-order meeting, and everyone was enthusiastic about embarking on the manufacturing and assembly of this new machine. I was very excited and proud about our success. I prepared a copy of the order documentation, along with the contract and final price and terms, to bring to our weekly meeting of senior management to show off our team's conquest of the initial sale. As it turned out, I forgot to keep one critical person in the loop about what we were doing—our CEO. I gave him a copy of the order documentation I had prepared at the meeting. He flipped through it and apparently was not overly pleased with the pricing we had agreed upon. He looked over the top of his bifocals at me and threw the three-ring binder toward me, saying, "This is a piece of shit!" All of the efforts over the last year suddenly turned from elation to disappointment. While I had received the endorsement from my boss and the bulk of the organization to make the deal, the head of the company had not been informed, He did not approve the decision, even though my direct superior had been aware of it. I never made that mistake again.

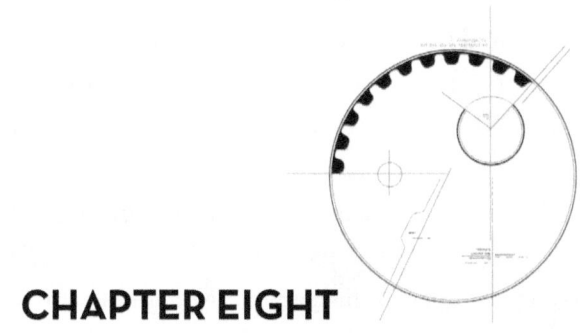

CHAPTER EIGHT

Communication Is King

Nothing is more frustrating than not hearing back from a request you sent in a timely fashion. It's like sitting at your gate at the airport looking at the flight status that merely says delayed, with no additional information. There is no excuse for not getting back to a customer in a reasonable time frame, even if it is to say that you need more time to process the request. Or a standard response such as, "I am out of the office and currently do not have access to the tools I need. I can process this in X number of days or you can contact my colleague, so-and-so, to handle your inquiry."

Always Reply Promptly

Most sales professionals have a cell phone, tablet, or laptop that are capable of retrieving voice mail or e-mail. There is no excuse, *ever,* not to give a reasonably prompt response to any and all requests. My personal choice is to respond with a phone call rather than a faceless e-mail. It is more personal, and you can learn more about the person and his or her needs in a brief discussion than you can from a toneless e-mail. It is amazing what can be gleaned from an actual conversation compared to swapping written messages. It takes longer than a quick e-mail, but I have found that when I engage in a conversation, I get a much better feel for the person I'm dealing with. A good rule of thumb is e-mail threads of more than two messages are usually better served by a conversation.

You may not be able to answer a particular inquiry immediately. If that's the case, you can respond with, "I'm working on it, but it may take a day or so," or "I will have this to you tomorrow," or "I need more input to ensure I get you the correct information." It is also imperative to take on personal responsibility for the inquiry. Do not pawn off a delay with excuses or a lack of response from a third party. This only complicates the situation and reduces your credibility. Assume complete responsibility even if you are hindered by outside entities.

Leaving E-mail Messages

As I have said before, my personal preference for an initial response is a phone call, but it is frequently difficult to reach someone by phone. Leaving a voice mail is not much more effective or informative than an e-mail, and sometimes an e-mail is an acceptable way to reply. I'll talk more about writing e-mails later, but keep in mind that even in an e-mail, it is important to convey your message concisely, with proper grammar. Many people have gotten lazy, ignoring the use of the shift key to capitalize the first word of a sentence, or using various shortcuts. Avoid the current fad of shortcuts and attention-getting formatting, such as all caps, no caps, or trendy acronyms (e.g., LOL). Many people are accustomed to these, but picky people get turned off by lazy prose, bad grammar, or overly used shortcuts. Why take the chance, particularly if you do not know the addressee personally? Much like dressing up for an initial meeting, no one will fault you for writing in complete sentences with appropriate punctuation.

I understand that the modern era of communication is e-mail or texting. While being technically savvy, I still prefer using the phone. There is no better way to get a read on a person than talking to them.

Exchanging e-mails frustrates me, offering little insight into the personality of whom I'm dealing with. I tend to respond to most e-mail inquiries with a phone call. I feel I get know a person better, including subtleties in their personality by verbal communication. E-mail threads can go back and forth, over and over, without a complete understanding of the issue on either side. The point is, respond as soon as possible and take full ownership of the request with appropriate professionalism, to show you are in charge. And make your response as clear, correct, and complete as you can. Otherwise, the inquirer may get a bad impression or, at worst, be inclined to look elsewhere.

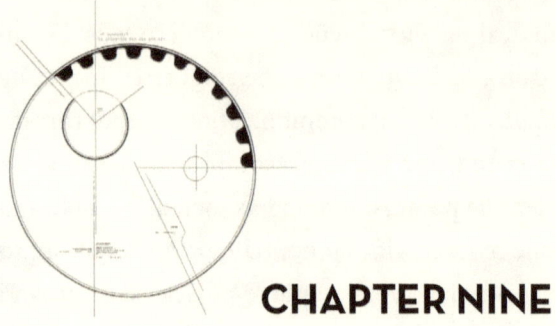

CHAPTER NINE

Dealing with Price or Delivery Resistance

Once you have established contact and open communication with the potential customer, the next natural step in the process is to respond to the customer's needs. A quick reaction time to a request will have a positive influence on your customer's receptiveness to your offer. Your cover letter or e-mail should include a summary of the discussions you had, why your offer is a fit, and what was done to arrive at the final configuration of the proposed equipment. This will help with the first impression of any offer. Be sure to follow up in a reasonable time frame (twenty-four hours is a guideline) by asking if the customer received the response and if it contained everything he or she wanted. Also, offer to expand on or change the proposal as required—but without making commitments you might not be able to deliver on.

Tweaking the Proposal

The next step in the process, after modifications and fine tuning, would be to discuss the submitted proposal. This will generally be a review of the technical specifications and a reassurance that the quoted scope of

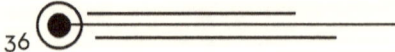

supply meets the customer's requirement, as well as what your company can deliver. If this leads to additional tweaks, then so be it. Just be positive that the final proposal is exactly what is required and is what you and your company are capable of.

However, shy away from a positive response to requests that you or your company can't provide with total confidence. Remain positive, but convey that it is important for you to ensure that the requirements they demand can be met. Remember not to respond to any request with no. Explain you are unsure and need to do more looking into the request, with a promise to respond in a specific time frame.

It's Their Job to Get the Best Deal

After you and your prospect agree that the quote meets their needs, the next step will be commercial discussions. This is especially true with capital purchases. Price, delivery, and terms of the purchase will all be placed on the table. Bear in mind that this is a natural part of the selling process, even if comes across as contentious. Try to remain calm, even if the suggested alterations seem completely ridiculous. Your body language and attitude will send signals as to whether or not the discussion is reasonable. An immediate rejection or even a heavy sigh sends a clear negative signal. You are better served by acknowledging the requested change as valid before making a counter suggestion.

While other issues arise in a negotiation, the principal ones are price and delivery. It is an extremely rare situation when a potential customer says "Hey! That price is reasonable!" or "What a great lead time you offer!" If you have done your homework before issuing a quotation, you can factor some cushion into both of these critical items. This can be trickier if you are in head-to-head competition with another supplier. Try to find out if this is the case before you even submit your quotation. If you cannot learn this, assume it is the case. You may also be negotiating with a purchasing person who was only on the fringe of the discussions about specifications and scope of supply. It is that person's job to get the best deal for the company from a contractual perspective. Prior to contract negotiations, whether with someone familiar or an unknown buyer, know what you have to work with. If you have prepared correctly, you should know how much wiggle room you have with price and delivery. This is especially true when dealing with customers in other countries, particularly Asian and Middle Eastern companies.

"I'll Get Back to You on That"

While patience is an absolute virtue in negotiations, there will be times when you reach the limit of what you can commit to. It's okay to say, "Sorry, but that is the best we can do." If there is still resistance, there is nothing wrong with saying," Let me work on that and I'll be in touch."

Another effective tactic is to divert the focus from the current topic—price, for example—and offer other value-added conditions to the order. This could be an extended warranty or perhaps some complimentary service or parts. These things will probably not be a price burden on your company. You'll have to read the situation or, more importantly, learn what is critical to your potential client.

Keep Your Cool

Just remember to always keep your cool and do not ever act surprised by any demand. Behave as if you expected the reaction and respond in an calm tone, even if you know the request is completely off base. And try never to be startled by either good or bad news.

I previously mentioned the negotiation for a project in Georgia for a new nylon recycling plant. When the purchasing agent announced they were not going to negotiate price because of all our efforts to get the process right, I had to kick my young salesman under the table to keep him from showing his pleasure. There were still details to nail down. Still, it was pretty cool when he let out that shout in the elevator on the way out. Just save your reactions—good or bad—for when the customer is not around … and when the deal is signed in ink.

You Never Know How a Deal Will Close

I was involved in a project in the Dallas, Texas, area for a plastic processing line with a major player in the industry. The order was worth more than $3 million. After almost a year of discussions, we were invited for the final negotiation. While we haggled over a few commercial terms and conceded a bit on delivery, we finished the meeting without a word about the price. We were invited to play golf at a Tournament Players Club course, where the company had a corporate membership. Once we were all checked in, we walked to the first tee. The project manager, who was handling all the negotiations, said, "How about a little wager on the round?" Figuring this was going to be a standard fun bet, I agreed. Come to find out, he wanted to play me and my colleague for 3 percent of the contract price in a match-play format. I had no idea how good a player he or his partner was, but I did know that I had the authorization to offer up to a 5 percent discount on the contract. After putting my head down, apparently in angst (I was actually smiling), I reluctantly agreed to the bet. We won the match and got full price for the contract. While this was an unorthodox method of negotiation (and the only one like it in my life), you never know how the closing of a deal will transpire.

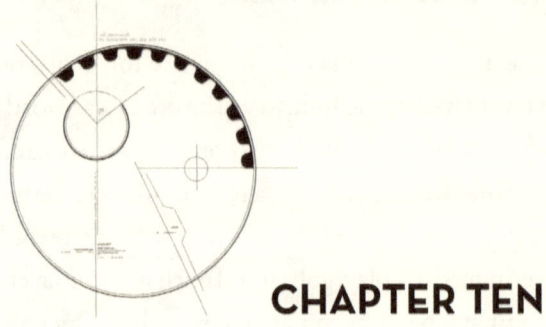

CHAPTER TEN

The Real Voice of the Customer

There are many buzzwords used in training quality-assurance professionals and salespeople, including *customer-centric*, *paradigm shift*, and *win-win*, to name few. Like the broad statement that "people only buy from whom they like," the term Voice of the Customer (VOC) is one of these buzzwords that is not the same in every situation. Actually, none of them are. If the term was Voic*es* of the Customer*s*, it would be more accurate. If you conducted a direct-marketing survey of companies you do business with to find out what they would like to improve, you wouldn't use only one customer's feedback to dictate how you operate your business or the products you offer. Every company is unique and has its own voice, so your question should be "How can I garner their confidence and get orders within *this* company's doctrine?" Get the company behind you with its unique VOC.

Rely on Your Research ... and Your Gut

I have never been a huge fan of metrics when dealing with the selling process. Considering that every situation is unique, it is best to rely on your research and knowledge of the customer, your experience and what

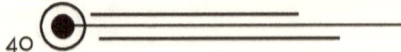

your gut tells you rather than some statistical analysis. Not to dismiss the value of knowing the market in general, but you should keep in mind that every situation is different, every company is different, and every opportunity for selling success is unique.

The VOC is still an important concept and can be used as a tool to determine what the customer desires, but it can also provide insight into better alternatives you may have to offer. Be aware of your company's capabilities, although there is nothing wrong with pushing the envelope, especially if the customer is looking for something new your company can actually develop and offer. Think of this as an opportunity to offer an alternative solution. If the particular demand is something many of your current or potential customers can also use, then it may be worth engaging your company in research and development to satisfy more than one customer.

Acknowledge the Customer's Request

Another VOC aspect is not product related, but rather relates to how the customer is supported, including customer service, spare parts, field assistance, and repairs. The first key to any and all responses to VOC is making the responses timely. Even if you don't have an answer yet, a simple "I'm working on it" goes a long way to show you have acknowledged the issue and you will get back to the customer as soon as possible. It's better still if you can provide a time line for the answer, but simply acknowledging the request goes a long way to establishing or maintaining credibility. There is no worse reaction to a customer inquiry than a nonresponse.

This aspect of the Voice of the Customer—timely response—is frequently overlooked when it should be part of the DNA of your company. If you are in sales management, it is essential to get this message across to anyone in your organization that has contact with a customer. It is important to make the customer aware that you are available to consult on any contentious discussions as well.

While the Voice of the Customer should not dictate 100 percent of your company's selling policies, it should absolutely be a factor in how you handle existing and potential customers. If you are in the midst of a selling discussion and you are asked for something unusual, "Why do you need that?" is not a good response. Rather, say, "I'd like to know why this information is important to your project so I can address the issue and respond with the best solution possible." Much better.

Service after the Sale

After-sales service is an essential part of any capital goods or industrial sales. It is important to have the same mantra across company lines for dealing with customers. In an organization involved with technical sales, after sales, spare parts, and service are usually handled by different departments. Any company that has different departments with access to customers should have a common culture and message. Any personnel involved with customer contact should have the training to respond in the same manner to any and all customer requirements, regardless if it is a new sale, spare parts, or a service request.

While consistency among company departments is important, it is equally essential for everyone involved with your customers to understand that they (the customers) are unique and should be treated as such. Some companies are driven by prices, others by delivery dates, others by quality concerns. Once that driver is determined, this information should be conveyed to anyone who has contact with the customer. This is at the heart of Voice of the Customer. When you receive an order, write a memo to all persons or departments that may have post sale interaction and provide a summary of the sales process, including key players, personalities, the buyer's tendencies, and any other pertinent information. Encourage addressees to keep you informed of any and all contact. Whether or not you carry that title, you are now the account manager for this customer.

When I was in charge of a global sales organization, I arranged for a sales meeting at one of the larger trade shows when a majority of my sales force would be in town. I prepared an agenda and a time frame for each topic to be reviewed, including updating product development, company goals, and how each individual could help the company be more successful.

Get Information from up and down the Company Ladder

For one such meeting, I asked in advance for everyone to probe customers about what they really wanted in a supplier like our company. Only a disappointing number of the field salespeople put any effort into this exercise, but some took the task seriously, and it showed when I asked each individual to tell everyone what he or she had found out. The majority focused on customers complaining about price, delivery, commercial terms, and slow responses to their needs. Not a single one had anything to report about the performance and reliability of the equipment or complications in operation of the equipment and maintenance. Knowing that the latter issues could only be gleaned from the people who actually operated and maintained the equipment, I concluded that all contact made with customers was done at a purchasing or management level. It is important to know a company's hierarchy and establish a relationship, but it is equally important to know the customer from top to bottom, especially those who have hands-on involvement with your product every day. Once you take all the information from up and down the ladder, apply a filter and give your sales force a well-thought-out dissertation of the big picture.

Despite having a mechanical engineering degree, I've spent the bulk of my time in technical sales, which I believe has helped me find out as much as possible—whether positive or negative—about what is truly important to the customer. You have to have a slight political bent to be a successful technical salesperson. Do not overlook anyone in the organization who can provide you with even a tidbit of usable information, whether positive or negative.

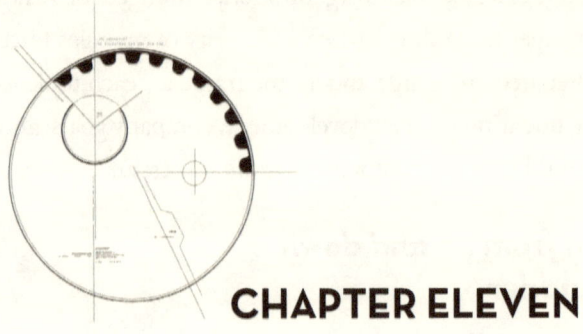

CHAPTER ELEVEN

Closing the Deal

Once you have taken the steps to learn about the customer, the competition, and the customer's requirements, hopefully you will be invited for one last discussion. Unless the customer tells you, you may not know whether this is the time to close the deal, but you should prepare as if it were. If you attend this meeting without knowing what you have to work with in terms of price, delivery, or other factors affecting the order, you might either lose the opportunity to finalize the deal or create a further delay that could open the door for other bidders to get their feet in.

Be Honest about Your Capabilities

It is incredibly important to maintain a receptive tone, regardless of the discussion, while remaining "real." Blowing smoke is so transparent to most people and is, frankly, a huge negative. Most customers mostly buy from people they like, but they will buy from someone they view as insincere even less frequently. You don't have to make statements you feel the customer wants to hear; you have to be completely honest. Once again, if you are unsure, do not fake a response. State your need to check on the request to ensure you have the complete backing of your company. Sometimes, this can be done on the spot with a phone call or text message during a break in the action. At other times, you may have to ask for time to gather information so you can give an accurate response.

The more elaborate and costly the project, the more discussion will be required to finalize a result. For example, some industrial products can be sold without a single face-to-face meeting and may be a one- or two-week process, ending with a phone call from the customer's purchasing department with an order. There may be a request for a price or delivery concession. If you can offer this within the confines of what you know is possible, it will help seal the deal in one phone call.

Larger Orders Take More Time

When faced with more elaborate capital projects, the process can take much longer. Other issues besides price and delivery can factor into the decision, including shipping terms, payment, warranty, and many other contractual terms—all the way down to the laws of what state or country will be applicable in the case of a dispute. The value of the order and the number of parties involved are directly related to the length of the process and the complications that will need to be dealt with before an agreement is reached. We see this regularly in the political arena. No matter how well-defined a proposal is, there will always be those who object to certain aspects of it.

Even Seasoned Salespeople Occasionally Sweat

When I was managing the sales department in one of my career stops along the way, we worked for over a year on a specific piece of capital equipment to be used to make the raw materials for lining and capping landfills. Our Houston office was the point on this project, handled by a seasoned veteran of our company, Ed Marshall. This was a $3–4 million order, and the client company was run by born and bred Texans. (Some might call them good ol' boys.) Ed had gone above and beyond to meet customer demands and close the deal, although there seemed to be no end to requests and concessions.

After going through this process for the better part of a year, Ed called me and informed me that my presence was requested at a meeting with him and the customer. He warned that this was usually a sign for further concessions or complaints about commercial terms, including price. This, despite the customer having whittled away our wiggle room through countless discussions, that included comparisons to competitors' offers, even though the customer never stated exactly what the other offers were. Upon arrival at the plant, we were escorted into the antagonist's office and prepared to do battle. We waited for about fifteen to twenty minutes, although it felt like an hour. Ed was sweating from the brow, which didn't make me feel very comfortable.

"The Man" entered and sat down behind his desk across from us with a surly look. He initiated the discussion by saying he had spoken with Ed and recognized they had already asked for many demands. He said they were no longer going to ask for more as they had come to a decision. He explained he felt it best to tell us in person. This all appeared to be the manly (read, Texan) way of delivering bad news. He then said, "I was not 100 percent accurate a moment ago. I did lie to Ed since I do have one more question that I'd like you to answer honestly." He spun around in his chair and reached into a refrigerator I hadn't noticed before. He extracted something and swiveled back toward us with a Cheshire-cat grin on his face. "This is my final question," he drawled. "What kind of Champagne do you boys like to drink?" And he displayed a bottle of Cristal in his left hand and Dom Perignon in his right.

Coolest deal closing I have ever been a part of. By the way, I went with the Cristal. Our previous antagonist opted for a Budweiser longneck. Ah, Texas.

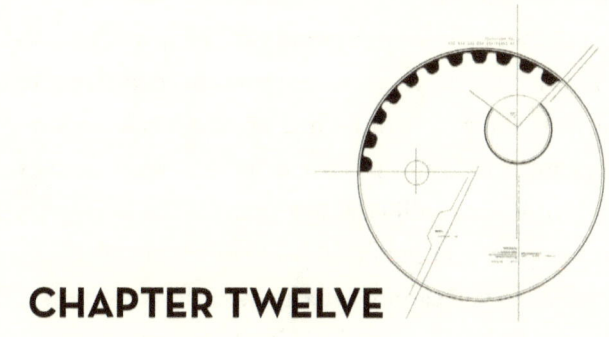

CHAPTER TWELVE

When to Say No

Once you have established rapport with the customer and have finalized the required scope of supply and specifications, you should be offered a chance to win the bid. While applying the previously mentioned negotiation tactics, there is a point to draw the line. This line is a moving target depending on the relationship that has evolved, as well as company doctrine. If it has been strictly business without any light discussions or demonstration of cordiality, it will likely come with the feeling that the customer will be less receptive to continued discussion. If there has been some easy banter, discussions about personal interests, and a casual lunch or dinner, the receptive meter will run higher. That is just human nature, which cannot be faked or completely covered up, no matter how experienced you may be.

When You Have to Say No

Know the guidelines of what is and is not possible from a company standpoint prior to the meeting. This can relate to options you can offer, such as technical documentation that might be required, terms of sale, or commercial issues, depending on what stage of the process you are involved with. If you are asked about a particular aspect and are unsure, but do not believe it is beyond your company's capabilities, say so. If you know for a fact, whether from previous experience or intuition, that you or your company cannot deliver on what is requested, say so. However, remember to keep a positive demeanor when doing so. "I'm sorry that is not within our bailiwick, but I may be able to help you find an alternative or someone who can fulfill your request" is a perfectly acceptable answer.

When you cannot agree to meet the customer's needs for a particular request, cordially explain it is not something you or your company is comfortable dealing with. Try to turn the attention back to the positive aspects of your offer so you do not lose too much momentum with a negative reaction.

Occasionally, *no* is the correct response. If you have been accepting and cordial throughout the discussions and the customer continues to pile on requirements, it is okay to draw a line in the sand. You can say that extra effort will require additional company resources or procurement of materials not factored into the original order, which will have a financial impact on completing the order. This may be met with a degree of consternation, but will more likely be accepted if you've given this explanation.

When There's Disrespect

Sometimes, but not frequently, you may be faced with a situation of disrespect. This generally occurs with purchasing agents or buyers who believe it is their right to play the king to your pawn in a buyer-seller relationship. During initial phases of the process, this may come across as trivial, but over time, the chasm expands to an us-versus-them situation. Everyone has a different threshold of when the line of disrespect is crossed. Salespeople need to be more on the wait-and-see side of things and remain as cordial as possible, but there is ultimately a breaking point. When this occurs (hopefully not too frequently), it is okay to excuse yourself from the discussion, explaining that you are not comfortable with the tone or content of the conversation. Anger is not necessary, but a brief statement of disappointment and a swift exit will make the point. In many such cases, you may receive a call or e-mail from another person within the organization, asking for continued dialogue and apologizing for the antagonist in the previous engagement.

Find a Middle Ground

Even if the customer is not being a power-hungry jerk or flexing muscle, there are still times when requests, even ones that are made cordially, cannot be fulfilled. This is easier to dance around in a nice way while explaining why you and your company cannot meet the new requirement. The sooner this comes out in the process; the better off both parties will be, since it gives everyone time to make adjustments. If this occurs in the final stages—like during a contract finalization—then it can be trickier. But if you made it that far, neither side will want to give up over a single issue. Try to be creative by offering an alternative and not being dismissive. The words "no way" or "that's impossible" should never be uttered, even if they are appropriate to the situation. There is always a middle ground acceptable to all concerned. Let the game play out with minimal reaction. You may be surprised at the ultimate outcome.

I once worked on a large project for a Korean petrochemical, a little operation called Hyundai. After going through the usual gyrations of attempting to match the requested specifications, including the sizing of the equipment and ensuring compliance with local industrial standards, we prepared an initial proposal. We were invited to their offices in downtown Seoul to discuss our proposal. Since I had spent a number of years dealing with different cultures, I felt comfortable with the upcoming encounter.

My boss, our product specialist, and I made the trip with a positive attitude about our chances.

When we arrived, we were escorted to a meeting room. Given the elaborate reception area and since we were in a super-modern high-rise, I was surprised how small the room was. The Korean team came in and greeted us. Once everyone was seated, the room became even smaller. Almost immediately, every player from Hyundai lit up a cigarette. The room was beyond uncomfortable and claustrophobic. Despite this, we hung in there. As we got through a number of discussion points, the chain smokers all started hacking and then spitting into their empty coffee cups. I was disgusted, but bit my tongue.

Soon after the hacking and spitting started, I looked at my boss and noticed he was slouched down in his chair, perhaps to alleviate the smoking and spitting as much as possible. The leader of the Korean team noticed the slouch and asked my boss to show some respect and sit up straight. My boss, who had spent the bulk of his career dealing primarily with Asian customers, was acutely aware of the different cultures. However, this was too much for him. He snapped back that it was offensive to us to watch everyone in the room—except for him, our product manager, and me—smoke, and for us to be exposed to so much cigarette smoke. And even worse, to hear and observe them all hack and spit into their coffee cups. He then suggested (demanded) we adjourn for the day and come back tomorrow, when the offensive behavior would be at least limited. My boss did offer not to slouch in his chair going forward, his one conciliation that I believe drove his point home.

When we reconvened the next morning, there were no empty coffee cups in front of our hosts and the amount of smoking was vastly reduced, allowing us to have a more productive discussion. We got the $14 million order, despite the tension created at that first meeting.

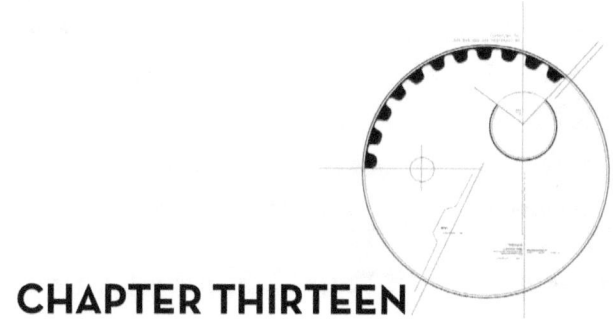

CHAPTER THIRTEEN

Treating Customers Right

As I said earlier, sometimes people only purchase something from people they like. While this premise is diminishing as a new world business order develops, it still shouldn't be overlooked. The days of the three-martini lunch, fishing expeditions, and golf outings are waning. But this does not lessen the importance of establishing a relationship with your contacts—especially if they have a significant role in the buying decision.

Your Challenge: Breaking Old Buying Patterns

It is not uncommon for organizations to purchase a product only from a specific supplier. This is especially true of certain entities such as suppliers to the government or the military, and large corporations. These sales become mindless, faceless, and lacking in any personal decision making.

With larger companies, especially those dealing with strict regulations or specifications, it can be almost impossible to get them to change a supplier, even if you offer an equivalent product at a better price with better features. Breaking this pattern may be one of the most significant challenge when calling on an account (More on this later.)

In some cases, even smaller companies are just as loyal to a particular supplier. If the supplier delivers what the customer wants, when they want it, and at a competitive price, they have no reason to look elsewhere. It is far easier to take the path of least resistance, for the engineer to specify and the purchaser to place an order with a long-standing partner. Remember the term *partner*. It will come up later.

Be Honest with Your Company Contacts

The larger the company you are dealing with, the more likely it is that you will not have direct contact with a decision maker. It is still important to develop a relationship with your principal contact. As trust increases, you can gain more information about the decision process of the organization. This becomes much easier if you actually like the person you are trying to convince to buy your product, and are honest with that person. Even the biggest egos or phoniest people have a sense of when they are being told the truth, rather than what you think they want to hear. So, while trying to get close to your contact, do not fake how you feel or what you think. The person you are dealing with will know, much a like a dog can sense feelings in humans.

Times have changed in terms of decorum and appearance. Generally speaking you can visit a customer wearing khakis and a golf shirt. But if it is your first time visiting, you should wear a shirt and tie. It is equally important, at the initial phase, to use Mr., Ms., Sir, or Madam when addressing a new prospect. When I'm addressed as Mr., I ask people to call me Mike, but I appreciate the respect shown. I often say, "Mr. Hotchkiss was my father. I'm just Mike." That can take the edge off and come across with sincerity.

A True Story about Good Customer Relations

Let me share a positive event that points up the importance of treating the customer right.

I was involved with a commissioning exercise (we called it a start-up) of the world's largest plastic-processing machine built by the Farrel Corporation. I had never seen a 10,000 HP electric motor used to power this monster, and I spent the better part of four months in Joffre, Alberta, Canada, for the installation. I had been on other start-ups, and they always had their difficulties, but not like this one. Much like a sales situation, they are all different.

This commissioning exercise was fairly comfortable, despite the typical twenty-hour days required for such activity. The customer, Novacor of Canada, was completely prepared to undertake the installation. No one ever got mad or disappointed when something went awry. They knew it would, as did I. Everyone from the plant manager down to the operators were totally professional and trained very well. Not the case in most start-up situations.

I became quite close with a gentleman who had emigrated from Eastern Europe and who was the primary engineer for the installation process. I even stayed at his house, and we rode bikes together, and went for a weekend skiing in Banff. It sounds like all fun and games, but I actually did work, on average, about twenty hours a day. After one such day—it was the middle of the summer—my new friend asked me if I wanted to play golf. I thought he was joking because it was nine thirty at night. He said, "Don't worry. We have at least two more hours of sunlight. We can get nine holes in easily." That is possibly the first and last time I played golf until eleven o'clock at night.

The moral of the story is: treat the customer with respect and you will, in most cases, get the same in return. While a grueling, stressful, and long operation, it was harmonious, and that made for a much smoother start-up.

In the midst of this successful start-up, we got the machine to run at 100,000 lbs/hr (40 metric tonnes/hr). This was the highest production rate ever achieved in a plastic-processing line. It made me proud to be a part of the team that helped make this happen.

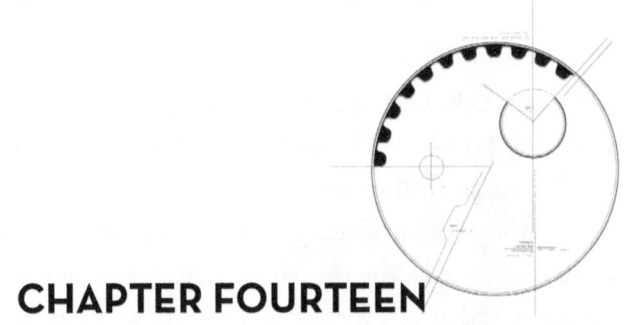

CHAPTER FOURTEEN

Earning Your Customer's Confidence

Once you have established a presence with the prospective client, the next step is to earn their confidence. This is a matter of establishing trust, delivering what is promised, and being likeable. You cannot achieve this by faking it, so you have to be yourself.

Effective communication is absolutely critical. At initial meetings, be even-keeled and positive, regardless of what topic is being discussed. The larger the audience, the more difficult this can be, as people have different opinions and personalities. Try to engage everyone you are facing. Even though you probably won't get to know each individual, you can still learn the company's goals and discuss them with a larger audience. Injecting humor or nonbusiness topics during the discussion can lighten the environment, provided it is not over the top. (Yes, political correctness is here to stay.)

As in life, you will not get everyone to like you or even agree with you, but it is possible to get them to believe you. This may require more than one visit, as well as following up on any questions or requests for information in a timely fashion.

Know What Makes Your Customer Tick

Winning someone over can be much easier once you know what makes that person tick. Does he have a large ego? What are his or her outside interests or hobbies? Where they live, and what is their family like? If they like to go fishing and you know nothing about it, ask them to explain what type of fishing they do. Remember, every encounter is different and should be treated as such if you want to be successful in gaining confidence. Eventually, you can weave in your own message about solving a problem your client's having or introducing a product that may help. But you can't do this unless you know your contact personally and what the client's company is all about. It is also difficult if you have not established trust before offering a viable solution to whatever the issue may be.

Don't Promise What You Can't Deliver

Regardless of the situation, do not make hollow claims about what you can do. In fact, it's better to undersell, saying you will get back to them later today or by tomorrow, and then provide an honest answer and honor the committed time frame. This is tied into the internal workings of your own organization. You can return to your company and get everyone on board who is required to make something happen. Then report back with confidence whether or not you can meet the customer's requests. If you cannot, do not make excuses or point fingers, just be frank. Your honesty will be looked at in a more positive light than if you had to retract a statement or a promise you made during your meeting.

Follow Up after the Meeting

"No news is good news" is about the worst possible philosophy to adopt when selling. A prompt follow-up to a meeting—whether with an individual, a few people, or a roomful of them—is critical to gaining or retaining the prospect's confidence. Do not underestimate the value of a thank-you note, recapping what you are going to do or reminding the customer they need to provide critical information. While a handwritten note is best, an e-mail with copies to all involved is perfectly acceptable. Starting an e-mail thread makes it easy for anyone in the loop to respond to everyone, with information that may be critical to the process exchanged on either side. Show interest and a humble thanks (assuming there is mutual interest).

Stay in Touch

Consistent communication is equally important. Keep your potential customer up to speed on all progress or setbacks as they occur in the technical sales process. It is highly unlikely that, when selling capital or industrial goods, you will have complete control over the entire effort. You must rely on internal sources, suppliers, and manufacturing or assembly scheduling to paint the full picture. Keeping your prospect in the loop of any changes or developments will help you gain credibility.

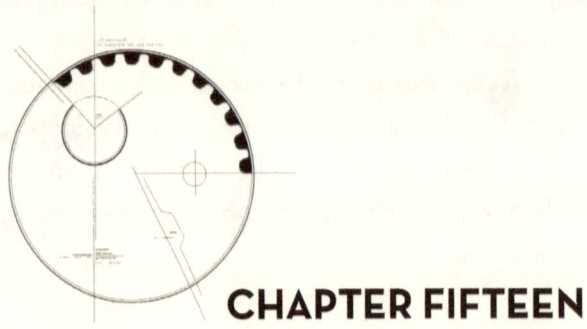

CHAPTER FIFTEEN

Establishing Rapport

You may have familiarity or perhaps even a history with a specific customer. This would most likely occur after months or years of cultivation and delivering on what was expected—on time and on budget. This does not happen overnight, so it is important to set a goal to make every customer comfortable with you and the products you offer. This sounds easy, but it really is not so simple. It goes back to the "buyers buying from someone they like" mantra.

Establish Rapport

You should automatically assume that initial and ensuing contact with a prospect will be entirely professional, with a certain arms-length philosophy. If you try to impress clients with your company's accomplishments, superior quality, customer service, and so forth on a first meeting, you may lose your contacts interest. They'll have a ho-hum reaction, easily observed by body language (yawning, fidgeting, and checking their phones or tablets). It is important to keep them engaged, and there is no better way to do so than to ask them about themselves and their company. After all, everyone has some form of ego. Try to find a common topic to start the dialogue. If you can't find any mutual interests, ask what their hobbies are, where they live, and what they like about the company they work for. There is a huge difference between a customer who is an active participant instead of standing around with hands on hips and pointing fingers. As a front-person, you can help to make it a partnership as opposed to a "we/they" situation. Always remember to engage and embrace a mutually beneficial relationship and avoid the typical supplier/buyer rift.

On some occasions, an individual may want to be all business. This is a different form of ego, where he or she can control the topics, tone, and pace of the discussion. Let it happen, and perhaps admire your contact's efficiency once engaged. What separates successful sales activity from unsuccessful can be the level of confidence you earn from the customer.

Follow Up to Their Requests

In addition to establishing rapport, it is equally important to follow up, in a timely fashion, to any requests or clarifications resulting from the conversation. There are many different ways of doing this. A one-line e-mail without a salutation or friendly sign-off may be a turnoff. It never hurts to include a brief statement about the encounter and the impression you took away from the meeting.

The follow-up can be difficult if you suspect the customer will not like the answers you have. Whether it is a technical specification, a supply of specific items, or commercial terms that cannot be met, ensure that the bad news is fully explained. Tell why you cannot do what was asked and pledge to offer an acceptable alternative. I hate this term, but it applies here: "Think outside the box," particularly if your box is small.

Maintain Post-order Contact

Once a level of confidence is achieved, it must also be maintained. If your initial contact goes well and your response was timely and cordial, it is important to keep this trend going. Remember that everyone is different, so the buttons you need to push to keep customers satisfied are most likely different from case to case. Although this is true, it should not preclude you from being who you are. It is merely a matter of being astute enough to recognize the subtle differences in every relationship.

Assuming you have been successful in establishing confidence and offering a desirable solution to the customer's needs, this does not mean you are done with your job. Following up is an imperative part of the process. In some cases, sales of major capital goods to the same customer occur one to three times over the course of many years. With industrial goods, this frequency can be much greater, but maintaining touch is vital in both cases. If you want repeat business, whether infrequent or establishing a regular pattern with the products you offer, it will largely depend on how you treat your customers after the initial sale. If you work for a large enough company, you probably have a customer-service department and a service department. Tell everyone who has post-order contact with the customer that you would like to be included in any and all correspondence to or transactions with that customer. You then should follow up to check the customer's post-sales experience and find out if there are concerns. If so, deal with them by letting the parties involved know what the negative response was and how they can do better the next time. A consistent organizational position is more likely to be viewed as stability.

No News Is Not Necessarily Good News

My favorite sales mentor of all time was a man named Clarence White who managed the field sales office in Houston, Texas, where I was based in the late '80s. I was still relatively new to the technical sales of capital goods, but full of confidence and bravado. Clarence was a tried and true Texan at heart, despite being born in the Northeast of the Unites States, so he had a bit of drawl, which added to his appeal. I never heard Clarence say a cross word about anyone or anything. He believed that positive thoughts bring positive results. He once asked me how a particular customer was doing, sometime after I had executed a sale. I told him I had not heard from the customer, so I assumed everything was okay.

Smiling, Clarence, said "Mike, there is no such thing as 'no news is good news' when dealing with a customer." Clarence continued, "I would argue the contrary, since no news means they may be looking elsewhere for help or support if they need it and you should find out." (He always addressed everyone by his or her name, sometimes the first name, sometimes Mr. or Mrs. So-and-So. The informal "son," "young man," "lady," "pal," or "good buddy" never passed his lips. A subtle yet effective personal touch that was his natural way. Then he added, so as not to appear to be admonishing me, "Go and give them a pat on the po-po and see what is going on."

I have never forgotten this sage advice from a white-haired and always smiling man, who wore a bolo tie and well-worn cowboy boots and was proficient at playing the banjo. And I continue to practice the law of "a pat on the po-po" to this day. Clarence White taught me most everything I needed to know about handling customers. The last time I saw Clarence was in a Houston hospital when he was on his deathbed. He was still smiling despite being fatally ill. Remember to remain positive regardless of the circumstances. Clarence did, and that was enough for me.

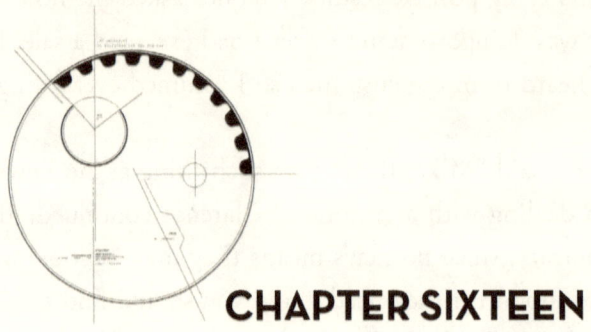

CHAPTER SIXTEEN

Do What You Commit to Do

You can only make so many undeliverable promises (like one or two) to become persona non grata within a target organization. It is critically important to submit to demands only when you are 110 percent sure they can be delivered. If this is beyond your control, then you may have to step back and get confirmation from whatever source you are not in control of. Often, you may be pressed to give an answer, but no answer is worse than an answer based on a lack of complete knowledge of what you are committing to.

In today's world, if the situation is urgent, you have many resources you can use to verify whether you can perform a requested task. If you're in a meeting with the customer, simply wait for a break (or ask for one) and make a few calls, text messages, or e-mails to see if you can obtain a quick answer. If this doesn't produce results, then table the request and commit to get back to the customer within a certain window of time. Just don't be disingenuous. People have internal meters that can smell a pile of BS from a mile away.

Know What Every Tentacle Is Doing

The core of the commitment issue goes back to knowing completely what is required and who needs to be involved to make it happen. This may include internal sources such as engineering, purchasing, operations, or certain critical suppliers. The entire selling process has many tentacles and, to the best of your ability, you need to know each tentacle and the role it may play. Being proficient at selling has nothing to do with your ability to be persuasive with a customer or making blind promises, but requires knowledge of the network you have to deal with and getting everyone on board with what you are trying to accomplish. Inclusion of these sources will ultimately help you to commit to what is required to win an order or even get your foot in the door. Exclude no one. Include everyone.

If You're Pushed to Do More

On a cautionary note, once you and your company establish that you are able to deliver what the customer requires, you may find yourself pushed to do even more. This goes back to my earlier suggestion to decline to say yes if you are not 100 percent sure. This is always better, while you promise to get an answer as soon as possible. Acquiescence is one thing, but lying down without complete backing and the knowledge of those with influence is far worse, regardless of the pressure being applied.

Commitments to prospective customers can include accepting a deadline to submit a proposal, or a contractual obligation agreeing on price and delivery. These are major parts of a technical sale for capital or industrial goods, but do not dismiss the commitment to a follow-up phone call, an e-mail, or any other seemingly mundane part of the selling process. Do what you say you're going to do! If this becomes a problem, than notify the other party that you need more time to answer the specific issue, no matter how trivial.

Stay on Top of the Process and Progress

When relying on others or outside sources for a response, keep track of their progress. The worst thing that can happen is to have a deadline arrive, the customer calls to check, and you do not know why there was a delay or even what the problem is. If you stay on top of the progress—whether it is a quotation, a technical question, or a required test to determine suitability—it is much better to give advance notice if there will be a delay. The only time customers should call you is to place an order or discuss interest in a product. When they call to inquire about a delay or problem, then you probably have not been paying close enough attention.

The worst case is if the customer starts reaching out to other people to get answers. This makes you look incompetent at best or lazy at worst. This is made even more punitive, because now you have a customer and a coworker or superior who needed to get involved because of a perceived shortcoming on your part. If for no other reason, which should be motivation enough for you to follow through on delivering expectations.

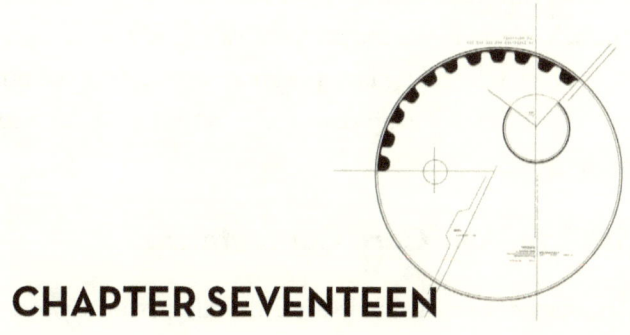

CHAPTER SEVENTEEN

Never Make Excuses

Along the same lines as living up to commitments, don't pass the blame on to some other person or entity for not responding as promised. Despite not having complete control over support, whether internal or external, pointing a finger to deflect any criticism won't maintain the confidence you might have developed. It is okay to say that there have been unforeseen delays. However, you must add "I will personally follow the situation until I can report on what you requested, ASAP." The next step is to find out what the problem is and convey this to the customer.

Keep on Top of Post-order Progress

Once an order is received, the next biggest faux pas is to not follow the progress of the order and keep on top of the schedule. Calling the customer on the scheduled ship date to inform him that the order is behind schedule is way too late. If you keep your finger on the pulse of the entire process, you should know when a delivery may be in jeopardy. This is the time to notify the customer. Again, if they are calling you, then you are not doing your job. Do not complicate the matter with another uninformed response to the new commitment. If possible, find out before you make the preemptive call so you can give advance notice of the new schedule. Have the answers ready for the questions they will ask about the new ship date and what is being done to try to solve the problem.

Stick to Your Core Competency

Another common thing I've heard a salesperson say to a customer is, "My boss says we cannot do that." How quickly can you say *loss of credibility*? If you point up the ladder as a reason why something cannot be done, your customer will ask to speak with the one putting up the roadblock. At the very least, turn this into: "As a company, we have determined that this is not something we should offer because it is not our specialty." Stick to your core competency while not being totally dismissive. On many occasions, you may be able to help the customer find what they are looking for, which is a far more credible response than blaming a superior or other source outside your control.

How many times when buying a new a new car, does the sales person say "I'll check with my manager" in response to some concession request? This does not give the sales person much credibility – at least in my opinion.

Be Punctual

Whether you are making a visit or having visitors come to you, be punctual. If you are paying a visit and are running late, get on your cell phone as soon as you know that you will be late and inform the point of contact. Showing up thirty minutes late without a heads-up already puts you behind in terms of reliability. The same is true if you are hosting and are detained at the appointed hour. Leave word with the receptionist or the client via cell phone, telling them of the unavoidable delay and the expected duration. If it can be arranged, have someone escort them to the designated meeting place and offer coffee, with the assurance that you will be joining them shortly. There is no worse feeling than sitting in an airport and staring at the dreaded *delayed* status of your flight, with no reason for the delay or an estimated time of departure. That's how it feels when an important meeting is delayed and you don't have any idea why or when your schedule will get back on track. Bear this in mind when you are detained from a meeting you are hosting.

Take Control If There's a Problem after Delivery

If a product malfunctions a short time after delivery and installation, don't make excuses to deflect the blame. If the problem is due to a purchased component or system, it is still best to take control by stating your commitment to get to the root of the problem. Save your admonishment of the supplier for when you speak to them directly; don't sound off to your customer. It's better to reassure your customer that you will get to the bottom of the problem and will report back as soon as possible with a resolution.

Again, the key is to keep personal ownership of the interests of the customer and to deliver what you have committed to, while remaining fully engaged with all aspects of the process.

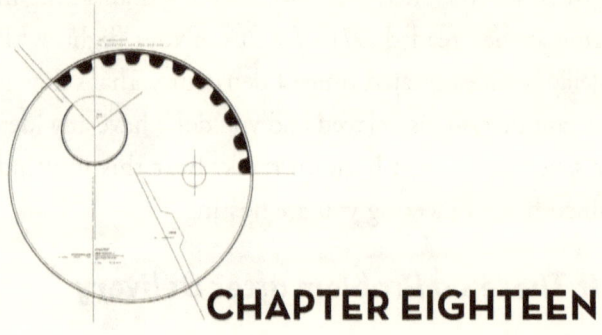

CHAPTER EIGHTEEN

Dealing with Problems

Disasters can occur, varying from severe loss of revenue, an industrial accident, or a personal injury, all of which qualify as major situations. I'm not talking about a busted knob, a squeaky bearing, or a minor component failing in its infancy.

Collect the Facts

Typically there are always glitches during the commissioning of a complicated piece of equipment. The problem may lie within items provided by suppliers that are not working as hoped, but are not under the direct manufacturing control of your company. Sometimes, the issue is mistakes made in manufacturing/assembly or installation, or it could be related to inappropriate service or the inappropriate use of the equipment by the customer. Do not jump to conclusions until you have all the available information! This is the trickiest situation you can face with a new customer, as emotions run high and the problem flies up the customer's ladder of hierarchy faster than a speeding bullet, most likely without complete facts behind what is being reported. And of course, no one will raise his hand and say, "It's our fault." Fingers will be pointed, shoulders will be shrugged, and uneducated opinions will fly, adding more roadblocks to getting to the root of the problem. All of which deters the progress of what needs to be done—to collect all facts possible, so intelligent evaluations can be made.

Don't Encourage Unfounded Opinions

Because these situations are extremely visible and get the attention of senior management, that can help impede the fact-finding mission. Getting all parties on the same page and working toward a common goal to find out what happened is like the US Congress passing a unanimous vote on a new law. In a case that truly qualifies as a disaster, things have to play themselves out with everyone digging into the problem. Naturally, this will produce many different theories as to the cause of the problem, but at least it gets everyone concerned in a joint discussion. An individual person, even a senior manager or a project leader, will not have enough clout to unilaterally dictate any course of action. It is better to sit back and absorb everything you can without interjecting opinions.

If the situation escalates to the point of legal counsel getting involved … Well, that's a subject for another book, and certainly outside my wheelhouse, even though I have been involved in product-liability lawsuits. It's best to let the legal experts handle it, while remaining informed and not engaging other parties in discussion. Never assume or make ungrounded opinions. Stick strictly to the facts at hand.

Make Sure the Right People Are Problem Solving

When I was in field sales based in Houston, I assisted in the commissioning of a $5 million plastic-processing machine at a major petrochemical plant in Illinois. Having decent knowledge of many aspects of the equipment and the subsystems, I was excited to undertake the challenge. Boy, was I in for a surprise.

I had been on a few commissioning jobs and knew there were going to be workdays that ran twenty-four to thirty-six, lots of pressure from the owner, and ultimately the satisfaction of watching a piece of equipment generate 50,000 lbs/hr of processed plastic material. Since we're talking about twenty-eight cents per pound of plastic in a 24/7/365 operation, you can do the math to discover the level of attention the new processing line received. (About $2.4 million per week, in case you don't have a calculator.)

Fast forward three weeks. After little sleep and a couple of major bearing failures in a $750,000 gearbox and mixing machine, we officially had a disaster on our hands. It had escalated to having all the senior management of both companies involved with plenty of the aforementioned finger pointing. The customer's plant manager had spoken to the CEO of our company to get his commitment to resolve the issue.

We were summoned to a conference room at the plant for a discussion. The contentious meeting lasted about four hours, with all parties involved, including the engineering contractor, the customer, the gearbox manufacturer, and the machine maker (yours truly), as well as all plant personnel. When the meeting ended, we had a more cordial attitude and a plan of action. The cost of the plan was still unresolved, but it was, at the time, less of a concern than getting the unit up and running.

As the meeting dispersed, the dyed-in-the-wool, Midwestern-bred gray-haired plant manager came over to me and put his arm over my shoulders. He expressed appreciation for the amount of effort expended thus far by the crew and disappointment that it did not go according to plan. He started chuckling and then laughed out loud as he said to me, "Son, it would be fun, I mean so much fun"—knee slap—"to have as much money as *your* boss and tell his customers to go fuck themselves."

I spent the better part of six months in Joliet, Illinois, to make this thing work. It eventually did, and the root cause of the problem turned out to be something simple—though that did not lead to an easy solution. It was discovered by a veteran maintenance manager looking at a technical book on mechanical devices from the 1950s. If the conditions are right, stray electric current from the main motor can pass through bearings, causing them to fail (10,000 HP exacerbated the issue). After spending hundreds of hours and hundreds of thousands of dollars, the problem was explained in a textbook that was over forty years old.

Dig in deep and get all the facts and keep the right people on the task at hand, not just the "suits" whose only intention is covering the company's interest and their own asses.

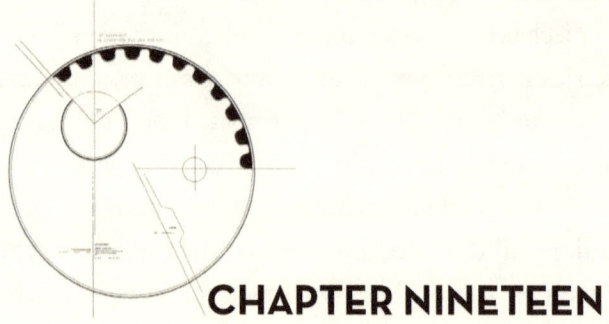

CHAPTER NINETEEN

Handling Angry Customers

Occasionally, you may be faced with an irrational or agitated customer. This is usually a post-sale situation when expectations have not been met, regardless of who is to blame. Often, the ire comes from someone who was not involved with the initial sale, but someone in a more senior position. Frequently an angry reaction is based on information fed to a customer by the purchaser or, more likely, the person who is using the product and having difficulties. Like the old party-line game, much information gets lost in transition. Remember to keep your cool and always be cordial and diplomatic.

A Sample Chain of Miscommunication

Operator to Foreman: "This thing we just installed doesn't seem to be working right."

Foreman to Operations Manager: "That new piece of equipment we just installed doesn't work as expected."

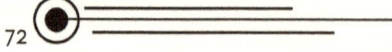

Operations Manager to Buyer: "That piece of junk you just bought is causing us loss of efficiency and money!"

Buyer to Purchasing Manager: "That new vendor sold us an inferior product that does not meet up to the performance we demanded and they verified they could deliver."

Purchasing Manager to VP of Operations: "We have a serious issue with a new vendor who did not do what was promised and now it is wreaking havoc on our operation."

VP of Operations to You (the sales manager supervising the sale): "We need to meet ASAP! You guys lied to us and delivered an inferior product that doesn't do what was advertised. Get your butt over here. We want this resolved immediately!"

You get the point. Nobody inherently wants to take the blame for a problem, especially if they do not have a clue as to the cause. Communications within a company and the company culture can play a huge role in how feedback is interpreted. Try to get to the root of the problem and don't trust the rant of a senior manager who works five levels away from the actual situation. Most of the time, there is a simple explanation. Usually, it's not even about the product itself, but rather the installation, operation, or maintenance practices over which you have no control. Once you find the root of the problem and can offer a solution or some advice, you can defuse the situation in fairly short order, even if you have to endure a rant first.

Take Ownership of the Problem

In the event the problem is related to your product or you misidentified the nature of the application, the best thing to do is to admit the wrongdoing and commit to fixing the problem as soon as possible. Information gives you the ability to speak with confidence about how to solve the problem, regardless of the source. You can graciously offer assistance without taking full responsibility until the root cause becomes certain. The cause of the problem is rarely as initially reported.

I was involved with a major petrochemical company and an entire project team, selling and subsequently manufacturing a $5 million processing machine. Numerous difficulties during the commissioning process led to a very contentious situation that wound up going to the top of both organizations. A meeting was organized to get some resolution to the problems—some, but not all, of which were our company's issues. Teams from both sides attended, including engineers, purchasing reps, and technical reps involved with the commissioning team (including me); about twenty people in all. My boss asked our CEO to make a cameo appearance to express his concern and support. After six or seven hours of heated discussions and much finger pointing, we eventually formulated a plan of action agreeable to both parties and, for the first time all day, there were smiles and even some laughter.

Just as we had agreed on a resolution, our CEO walked in to pay his respects and, I thought, to express his understanding of the gravity of the situation and our company's resolve to help fix the problem. Rather, he stated that our customer needed to take some responsibility for the problems. That threw seven hours of discussion and debate over responsibility out the window. The team of people representing one of our largest customers got up and walked out of the room. It took a few more trips and a large sum of money to resolve the conflict, but it was far more difficult given the contentious relationship created by the few words of the ego-maniacal leader of our company, who'd been unwilling to take ownership of the problem solving.

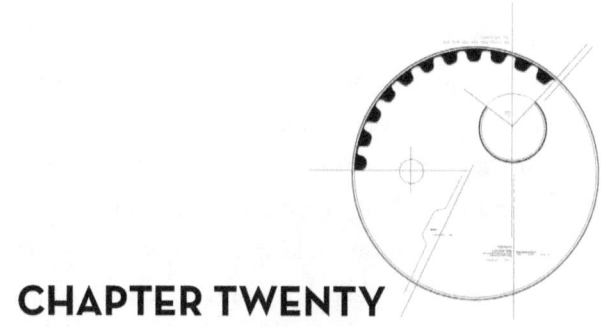

CHAPTER TWENTY

Handling Comparisons to Competitors

W hen your product or company is being compared with a competitor, bear in mind that dismissing or criticizing the opposition rarely works. By human nature, most of the people you deal with will not willingly dismiss a presumably equal product without being convinced yours has a distinct difference or advantage. They key is to demonstrate the advantage in dealing with your company as opposed to what they may be accustomed to. This goes back to the common denominator of doing homework and understanding what is most important to the customer. The rule of thumb in Marketing 101 is to offer the same product at a lower price. A preferable solution would be to offer a better product at the same price, or to offer a product unlike anything else available, provided its uniqueness makes it more desirable with better performance, longer life, and durability.

Don't Make Comparisons with Your Competition

Rather than claiming to have a better product, it is far more effective to promote the entire package of what you can offer, extolling the benefits rather than comparing, even if a comparison might be in your favor, to

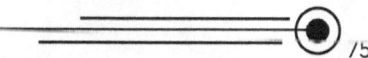

win over the confidence of the customer. Remember, you are selling the hole, not the drill. Knowing where the hole is going, the frequency of new holes required, and the specifications for the hole are tantamount to promoting how you can make the best hole.

You may come across prospects that have loyalty to a competitor stemming from a long-standing relationship. People tend to do what is familiar as opposed to making a change. It is often difficult to elicit a change, especially if there is a long-term relationship and familiarity with a supplier. You might find it difficult even to get the prospect to consider an alternative if they are satisfied with what they are using. Given this situation, the most effective way, unfortunately, is to offer lower pricing or better delivery or other desirable incentive(s) that your competitor does not currently offer.

Know What the Competition Is Offering

The other situation you may be faced with is a new project or sale where there are specific price and delivery expectations. In this case, of course, price and delivery play a crucial role. However, not all individuals or companies buy strictly on these factors. As a matter of fact, if these are the only criteria applied to a buying decision, then that company will not be very successful. This is why it is imperative to sell the value you offer and not just a price tag.

First, learn about the competitor's product and offer. Finding out about your competitor's pricing is tricky, since you cannot come out and ask directly and still maintain integrity. Besides, the comparison may not be apples to apples. If your products have certain discernible advantages, be sure to emphasize these differences, but do not put your competition down. Just extol the features, services, and support your company offers. This is why it is important to know as much as you can about the competitive product. Without pointing out a weakness in a competitive offer, you can promote the strength in your product that may be lacking in the other offer.

As important to the product itself is selling the entire support system behind it. It is an important topic to introduce, assuming your company has a solid after-sales support structure. If you keep critical spares in stock, mention that. Discuss your practices, including breakdown and critical-service policies. Ensure that you will personally be involved in tracking all their needs and that you have the ability to spur others in your organization to urgency if required.

The odds are, if you are thorough in learning as much as possible about a competitor and, more importantly, their offer, you will have an edge. While it's not wise to reveal what you know directly to the customer, you can still use the information in your favor with subtle statements or questions about the customer's desires in a partner for a particular project.

Most savvy buyers will not reveal details about competitive offers, but it is possible to learn a bit about the way they are leaning. All the classic terms such as price and delivery can be determined by asking questions and knowing the company you are dealing with. Having a read on what the competition is all about allows you to tie the story together and create a strategy to appear more favorable.

Offer an Extended Warranty

The most overrated term of a sale is warranty. The standard warranty in most sales is one year from date of shipment, and for manufacturers of capital or industrial products, this is a typical time frame. Warranties generally protect the user against defects in material or workmanship. Any manufacturer worth its salt would preclude this from occurring by a quality-control system, checks and balances, and testing prior to shipment. If there is a defect from the manufacturing process, this will generally show itself within the first week or so of operation. This can be termed *infant mortality* and rarely occurs. If it does, you simply honor the warranty. If something happens within eleven months, it is probably not a defect, but an outside influence that has created the failure. So why not offer an extended warranty as a bargaining tool? Warranties are conditional. Just check any automobile supplier. Offering an extended warranty shows confidence in the product you are selling. Your competitors may not see it that way, which can give you and your offer an advantage.

Appliance stores, electronic stores offer paid-for extended warranties. This is a bright marketing idea because very few claims will be made beyond the standard warranty period provided it is a quality product. While you cannot get away with selling an extended warranty for your product, it can be perceived by customers as a tremendous plus in your favor.

Sell the Benefits of Your Own Product

To get the order, apply the classic industrial or capital-goods technique of connecting the three sides of the triangle: customer, competitor(s), and your company's willingness to make concessions. Know the customer's DNA, know what the competitor's products and capabilities are, and have the ability to upward sell in your organization, so you can get everyone in agreement with what needs to be done to win the order.

In order to break through to a potential customer who only knows and uses products from the competition, you must sell the features and benefits of your company's product. It is folly to draw comparisons to the competitor, especially in a negative way. Stick to the product you are pushing, and draw the customer's attention to the benefits of the equipment you are offering, not the advantages you may have over alternatives. The difference being, benefits are specific to your product while advantages are comparisons. No one can argue a proven benefit, but we all can be subjective about proclaimed advantages. Also, sell the organization behind what you are offering, such as delivery capability, technical knowledge of your product, post-sales support, and the availability of spares and service. By probing in the initial stages, you can learn what is important to the individual you are dealing with and his or her organization. Typically, if you are still in the race, commercial issues will arise. Don't cave to every demand or request, but show a willingness to work with the customer's wants. Lowering your head and shaking it shows your disdain about working with your prospect. Accepting every suggestion with a positive statement will help to work toward a common ground—even when a suggestion is outrageous.

Real-Life Lessons

I was working with an agent in Korea with a major petrochemical company. It was a three-machine order for about $16 million. The technical side of things, while it took quite some time, went smoothly, and we had come to an agreed scope of supply.

Now the commercial discussion ensued. The original demands were so far astray from what was realistic; I must have visibly shown my reaction. During a break, our agent, who was a very sharp guy, told me that in the Korean culture, the worst response to a request is *no*. I have never forgotten that and have applied it to every negotiation since then. It is better to start with "I understand what you are looking for and it makes sense for your company, but have you thought of this alternative?" It is important to remain calm and appear interested rather than be reactive and antagonistic.

In a different situation in Taiwan (with Formosa Plastics), we were coming down the home stretch and knew the only thing left to do was to settle on price. We were brought into the elaborate and ornate office of the head of purchasing. After exchanging pleasantries and sipping some tea, the man in charge asked, through a translator, what the current cost of steel was per kilo. (We knew he probably spoke and understood English.) Our agent whispered the price to us. The head of purchasing then asked how much the machine weighed. Regardless that the equipment consisted of literally tons of exotic metals, materials, intricate manufacturing techniques, and complex prepurchased components, we answered with an estimate of the total package weight. He then, through his translator, offered to pay us 10 percent more than the going rate of steel for the total kilograms of the machine.

How do you respond to that? You don't. Just show respect and appreciation for the time allowed to meet with him. A gratuitous compliment, such as how well the organization is run—no matter how personally distasteful—is a positive way to end an otherwise meaningless meeting. Chances are you will not cross paths again with this person, but he or she may have a say in the final decision, so do not leave a bad taste in anyone's mouth.

CHAPTER TWENTY-ONE

Post-order Issues

Now that you have done all the background work and put much effort into ensuring the customer requirements and technical specifications are agreeable, you may now be given an order. Patting yourself on the back and congratulating those involved is a natural reaction to a job well done. The issue is this: the job is not done yet. You may hand off all the documentation to internal parties to execute the order as received. In many if not most cases, you'll get back requests to make changes to the order. The more complex the order and the more parties involved in the process, the greater the odds of change requests after the process is under way. It is very important to keep your finger on the pulse of the progress of the order and what influences may alter the original scope of supply, delivery, commercial terms, or anything else that might have come up since you finalized the order.

Clients Can Change Their Minds

Whether a smaller order for an industrial product, an engineered package, or a significant sale of capital equipment, the desires of the client can (and will) change. The first part of the process is receiving an order and going through an enter-order process, creating the equipment to the letter of the customer's request. Despite having countless sessions to make requirements abundantly clear, the actual order may contain something unexpected. That is why it is essential to review, in detail, all the order documentation generated during the process.

If there is a discrepancy or something has changed that was not mutually agreed on, it is important to take ownership of dealing with the customer while keeping your team in the loop. If you were successful in establishing trust and gaining your customer's confidence, then you will most likely be able to resolve any disputed issues.

Negotiate Order-Entry Issues Honestly

Once any order-entry topics have been resolved, sit back and wait for the changes to come—usually right after you have embarked on the part of the order that needs to be changed. Whether this is a technical or commercial issue, the only way to deal with it is head-on, with complete honesty. This may involve some internal negotiations, since the people in your organization who will be affected by this change are the ones who will probably complain the most. That is just human nature.

Try to get a complete assessment of additional resources, time, or cost that can affect the order as a result of the requested change. Most salespeople use the phrase "No problem" far too frequently. Be sure to do all the spade work to determine what the issues are and what impact they will have on the fulfillment process within your organization. Then you will be prepared to respond to the customer, and to be clear and honest, especially if the change will influence price or delivery. Be ready with an explanation why, and perhaps even explore alternatives to achieve a similar result that would have lesser impact on price, delivery, and maybe even performance.

When New Requests Are Put on the Table

As thorough as you may have been during the preorder process, be sure to remain even-keeled when alterations are requested that were never put on the table. Chances are, when this occurs, you may be dealing with a different person than your principal contact, perhaps a purchasing agent or someone else who was not involved in the entire preorder process. This is why it is important to remain patient and not get frustrated if you have to rehash issues previously gone over ad infinitum. You may find yourself resending information that had been agreed upon by both parties some time ago. If so, include a cover letter or description of where this information came from and why the change will have an impact on fulfilling the order without monetary or time consequences.

Sometimes It's an Internal Issue

There is also the occasion when a post-order problem is an internal issue. The order may not have been entered properly, the design department may have misinterpreted a specification, a supplier screwed up, or someone just plain made a mistake. This is trickier to deal with since you are now the bearer of what could be bad news. Do not sugarcoat the situation or point fingers in any direction. Assuming you have already established trust, an accurate assessment of the impact is always the best course of action. As with most situations with a customer, it's always best to have this conversation as soon as you are aware of an issue. Sweeping things under the carpet or nondisclosure are far worse tactics.

CHAPTER TWENTY-TWO

Dealing with Your Inner Circle

Often, some of the biggest roadblocks in the selling cycle are inside your own organization. Perhaps a micromanager or another salesperson feels he or she has a right to the potential sale. This can be trickier to deal with than winning over a customer because there are more politics involved.

I Agree, But ...

Upward managing is a touchy situation. While you may be passionate about a particular sale or project development, your boss may consider the effort or potential is not worth it. I have found that optimism and enthusiasm can overcome some of these doubts, but not always. Sometimes, you have to present a plan that shows the value for the company of pursuing a certain project. This may require making an argument with a well-prepared, understandable spreadsheet or other information, perhaps even an outside reference from a business or news outlet.

Outright disagreement with your superior will get you nowhere. If you are married, you know how this works. It is more effective to agree and then add a "but ...." In other words, express your opinion of the situation without disagreeing with the boss. If you're really good, you can convince your boss that his or her strategy for making adjustments is brilliant. In other words, check your ego at the door.

Speaking of egos, I was supervising a sales team in Houston while based in our Connecticut headquarters. We were having some issues with a customer who was being handled by Pete, one of our salesmen in the Houston office. When I visited the Houston facility on a routine check-in, I asked to organize a meeting with the troubled customer. I found myself alone with this customer, since the primary contact dealing with the problem had to take a phone call. Once we were alone, the customer stated with a laugh, "Gosh. I would love to have a dime for every dollar Pete thought he was worth. I wouldn't have to work anymore!"

I knew Pete had an ego without much to back it up, but this was a difficult situation. Upon a short reflection, I told the customer that he could contact me at any time regarding any issue. Without saying as much, I fazed Pete out of the picture. He never noticed. He was too busy telling other customers how great he was.

Just like customers can tell a BSer a mile away, they can sense an over-the-top, unwarranted ego two miles away. This just as much if not more of a turn-off than the BSer.

Again, Take Ownership

Many times fellow employees who report to you are influenced by you. Employees, even those of high rank, respond to demands either with willingness to please or the fear of reprimand. Any supervisor worth his salt would never use the rationale that "this comes from above." That is a lame explanation and, frankly, shows weakness. Just like dealing with customers, take ownership of any situation. It is hard, but it demonstrates confidence and will ultimately pay off.

Inside Impediments to the Sales Process

Other people in your company may be part of the sales process and may actually impede the process. It can be an internal salesperson, engineer, production person, purchasing agent, or manager of another department. Selling is not exclusively about the customer, and often the internal selling can be more difficult than dealing with a demanding customer. So, it's important to get everyone on board with your mission. The other salesperson may say, "We cannot get the quote done in that time" or "The delivery requested is not possible." The engineer could tell you that, "We haven't done that before. It will take time and be very difficult." The production manager may claim that the equipment cannot be built in time or explain how difficult (close to impossible) this potential project could be. The purchasing agent might say that the items required cannot be delivered in the time frame you committed to and, perhaps, that the quoted price is not sufficient to cover the cost of procured items. Other department managers may have objections too, ranging from the terms of sale, payment terms, or delivery requirements. Negotiations are not exclusive to the buyer you are targeting; they include internal discussions, communication, and understanding of the selling process and post-order activity. If you go rogue, you will undoubtedly have a bad sales experience pre- or post-order—or worse, both.

The important point is to recognize that the technical sales process is complex and requires taking into account many different factors, including the influence of your own organization on your efforts. Try to keep your fellow colleagues informed of developments and strategy with the customer and, most importantly, let them know they are a crucial part of the process. Resistance is often due to not feeling they were included in your selling activity. (Of course, keep any of these issues to yourself when facing the customer. Do not blame any shortcomings of the process on the internal workings of your company. As humbling as it may be, it is best to take complete ownership of the customer interaction without excuses or finger pointing.)

A Hard Lesson Learned

I learned an important lesson when developing a new product with an external company. This was done largely in a vacuum, because we were trying to design and build a product we had never built before, and our potential competitor owned the majority of the market for this machine. After a year or more of development, with very few people in the company aware of our efforts—which we called Skunk Works®, after Lockheed Martin's famous secret development program—we were ready to unveil the new product at a huge trade show in Chicago. I had developed manuals and sales materials for our sales staff, but did not disclose the nature of the release until a preshow meeting. The product was received with enthusiasm since our sales team was tired of going against a competitor with a huge market and no real competition. Once the word got out, the other people in the company, particularly the research and development and engineering departments, were not so enthusiastic about not being included in the development process. Hence, they had little to no willingness to support the new product. Despite being competitively priced and a superior product to the competition, it failed. Not from market acceptability, but from lack of internal support. We should have consulted Lockheed about how they handled that. Lesson learned.

Lockheed Martin's Skunk Works® was their top-secret Advanced Development Program. It was named after a moonshine factory featured in a "L'il Abner" comic strip.

Well-known successes were the U-2 and SR-71 Blackbird reconnaissance aircraft (top speed and altitude still classified), and the F-117 Nighthawk and the F-22 Raptor, now seen in many movies. The most current project is the F-35 Lightning II.

CHAPTER TWENTY-THREE

Selling through Field Sales and Inside Sales

Managing the sales process with internal resources is a different challenge. While you have more control of the process, like making demands, it still requires sensitivity to the other people involved. It is equally important to maintain interest and complete knowledge of the goings-on. You should empower those in your charge to take control and, at the same time, keep you informed. There is nothing wrong with making suggestions or even invoking your years of experience, but individuals on the front line need to feel ownership of the process.

Motivating an International Sales Team

Motivating the sales team is also different when dealing with internal sources. First of all, the fact they are working for the same company and getting paid to do so should be enough impetus for them to perform to expectations. In some cases, commissions may be used for further incentive, but either way, positive reinforcement will always be a strong and useful tool to help the salespeople succeed—that is, get the order.

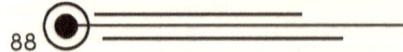

Communication is a good plan in just about every situation. Ensure there is an interactive channel between all those involved in an endeavor so that everyone is on the same page. Duplication of effort, sending different messages, or making statements to customers without everyone being in the know will make you look like a disjointed operation. It is not necessary to organize multiple status-update meetings, since current modes of communication make it easy to instantly share thoughts and results. Actions should not be taken unilaterally. Include everyone involved and get them on board prior to making any moves.

Keep Everyone in the Loop

If you are managing a sales process that uses your internal sales force, it is your job to keep the organization apprised of developments and how they can affect different departments. If the customer has a unique technical demand, be sure to consult engineering. If they have commercial demands other than the usual, whatever that is, you may have to run it by accounting or even a legal consultant. If there are demands on delivery or other issues that can affect production, consult operations.

I hark back to our nylon-recycling project. As this was something nobody had done before, countless hours were spent in the process laboratory with a variety of permutations to get the best possible configuration. There was a time constraint invoked by the investors funding the project, as well as an engineering contractor with a three-ring binder full of specifications and standards to be met. This was an all-in situation that required orchestration of the entire company. I have to say that if it wasn't for keeping everyone involved with ongoing information, the project and the significant sale would not have happened. But it did.

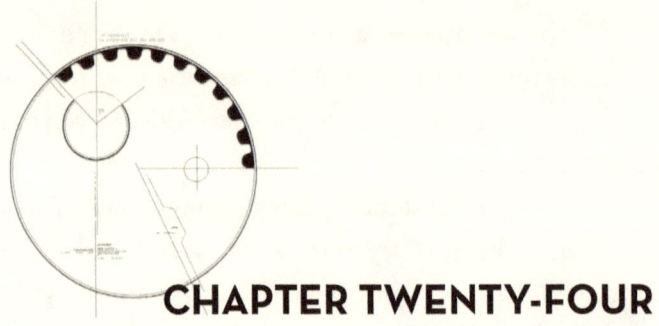

CHAPTER TWENTY-FOUR

Selling through Agents and Distributors

Many companies that manufacture industrial or capital products use a network of representatives or distributors to help sell their products. The only motivation for such entities is to make money. The way they make money is to close deals as quickly and easily as possible. The path of least resistance rule applies to most of those acting as sales agents for your company. If there are perceived roadblocks to making a sale, it is not likely to happen. Products that require effort, knowledge, and technical capability are harder to sell, so an incentive to do so is one of the challenges of selling through outside sources.

Agents

An agent is not an employee of your company, but usually is an independent contractor and thus is more receptive to guidance rather than orders. Agents are selfish in a way, as they are in it for themselves. But they can be influenced if they're convinced there is a deal coming along with a good commission. Keep in mind, their sole objective is to make a sale. If they sense this is only a distant chance, they will move on to a better opportunity. So, it is essential to keep them engaged if

 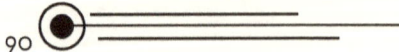

the opportunity is real. You have to rely on an agent's feedback to learn about the chance of success, so it is a bit of a motivational juggling act to get the desired information and discern how hard to push to advance the process. There is nothing wrong with pulling the plug if the opportunity appears to be hopeless and letting the agent move onto another possibility.

Distributors

Distributors are a bit trickier. They have a boss, work for a company, and are assigned goals. Commissions come from their employers, and their personal success is tied to what products can be sold in the easiest and most expeditious fashion. If they have another priority, it may be very difficult to turn their focus to your situation. It then becomes important to treat them like a customer and cater to what will motivate them to work on an opportunity you deem worthwhile.

It is imperative to get to know the distributors of your products. Though it can be hard to manage distributor representatives, you can guide them to become enthusiastic about a prospective opportunity. If they are committed, they can be convinced to put in the effort needed to gain the endorsement of their company. The best motivational tactic is to get them completely enthusiastic about the product and the company. You can't fake this. It requires that you sell the advantage of a product and how it can help them offer a solution no other supplier can. Do not oversell or blow smoke. Leave that to used-car salesmen and Realtors (appologies for the generalization). If you cannot convince someone of the advantages of your product in a real way, then you will lose every time.

Whether using a company salesperson, agent, or distributor, it's important to get know the prospect as much as possible prior to engagement. The Internet has made this task much easier. Not only can you view the potential customer's site, but also related sites, such as industry-specific trade websites, social media, or information from a trade publication. This is just a starting point, and you'll need to do more information hunting on the ground to become fully prepared.

Motivate Your Outside Agents

One source of motivation is to get the ones on the front line excited about the products they are selling. Some agents are curious and self-motivated, but that is not the norm. To improve anyone's enthusiasm about selling your products, it is absolutely necessary to demonstrate your own belief in the products you want the second party to sell. Frequent communication and demonstration of support are paramount. Give a detailed and positive description of your products, especially as they may relate to a given project. Be sure to provide requested information in a timely fashion. Just like dealing with a direct customer, stay in touch and keep agents informed of the status of your response. If you cannot reply in a reasonable period of time, touch base and advise when you can offer a response. Silence is the worst form of communication.

One other factor in selling through intermediaries is understanding what their goals may be vis-à-vis what your company can do. Words from the second party such as "I need this tomorrow" or "The price is too high" may be met with disdain from whomever is trying to make the sale. Much like dealing directly with a potential customer, starting with a negative response is not likely to induce perseverance in the middle party. Remember, you are probably not the only account he or she is working on, and an agent will always take the path of least resistance. Make yours the easiest if you can with quick and honest responses. Be honest, but never promise what cannot be delivered. It takes more patience and time, but understanding what is being requested and why will help you to project a positive outlook even if the demands cannot be met.

Make Them Look Good

Praise and timely support also provide motivation. Make it easy for the distributors or agents to look good to their prospects, and then praise them for their diligent effort. There are few things more frustrating than contacting a potential supplier for current price and availability and waiting days for a response. Let the distributors or agents know the time frame required to respond to an inquiry—the faster the better—and be sure to meet that commitment. If something arises that doesn't allow this, let them know sooner rather than later. Often with capital and industrial products, there is a reliance on outside sources to put a quotation together. If you are unsure of your suppliers' response time, inform the agent, distributor, or customer that you will get back in touch with a time commitment.

Information Gathering Is Still the Key to the Sale

When generating a proposal for anyone, ask as many questions as you need so that you are fully informed about the application. This is more important when selling customized industrial and capital goods, since it is rare for applications to be exactly the same as something done before. It is equally imperative to gather as much information about the commercial climate of the potential sale. Is delivery an issue? Is it price sensitive? How many competitors may be involved? Does the end user have any other expectations regarding warranty or payment terms? This seems to be a relatively simple thing to ask for, and it is if you are the one working with the end user. But using an intermediary can be more of a challenge because the intermediary often receives a request by e-mail or a brief phone call, and few details are offered or asked for. Explain the importance of gathering information to the agent or distributor and how it translates to their chances of closing a deal. Having as much knowledge up front, even prior to engaging in the order process, can mean the difference between success and failure.

Make Sure They Understand Your Product Inside and Out

It's important to train the people who are promoting and selling your company's products. This is best done face-to-face, but Internet meeting sites can work as well. Ensure that what your company offers is clear and understood. Go into details like typical deliveries, spare-parts availability, and service capabilities. Back this effort up with frequent communications, such as newsletters or e-mail to: (a) maintain a presence for you and your company and; (b) keep agents and distributors apprised of recent developments, including product updates and success stories. Be sure that all support materials are made available. In many cases, it is a good idea to have an exclusive section of your website dedicated to agents and distributors, which can include current pricing, company news, or detailed product information they can share with new prospects. Relationship maintenance is crucial to improving your ability to get orders.

CHAPTER TWENTY-FIVE

Marketing Industrial and Capital Products

Whether it's a personal visit from you or an agent/distributor, an e-mail, a direct letter, a well-organized website, or even a chat room, different customers react differently to different marketing tools and techniques. I believe in giving any and all potential customers their choice of contact method. There is no reason not to offer all available options for making contact, and it costs very little to offer different ways to communicate.

Preparing Your Mailing List

Have a specific target audience when preparing a mailing, bulk e-mail, or phone list. Gather the information about the targets and organize them in a database or spreadsheet. When marketing by old-fashioned mail, you can create a letter that is personalized with readily available mail-merge features. Try to get the name of a contact, even if you don't know if it's the person who will be the key to entry. If you're contacting a potential client via phone, saying "I'd like to speak to someone in purchasing" or

"May I please speak to the president or owner?" will be received with the same reaction you give someone trying to sell you loans, investments, or a "free estimate" for some service over the phone. Targeting your contact should apply to all forms of bulk communications. You will find, with a little work that your list will be reduced dramatically and your rate of acceptance, at least of starting an initial dialogue, will be much higher and therefore worth the extra effort. Document any and all responses— negative, positive, or indifferent—in your list, database, or whatever form you choose to keep track of who you're contacting.

Don't Force a Fit

Receiving any response can be considered a success, but in no way does it guarantee a return on your efforts. Find out quickly whether or not the new opportunity is valid. If it's not, politely move on while acknowledging your appreciation for the response. The point here is not to force anything that doesn't fit. You do not want to be the square peg talking to someone who needs to fill a round hole. Few things are more annoying than having an unsolicited contact, especially when the person calls on the phone, not taking "I'm not interested" sincerely. In my house, this leads to me hanging up the phone or even becoming cross with the unknown caller.

Cold-Calling

Cold-calling is very challenging, but sometimes can be a useful tool or can provide information otherwise unavailable from other sources. Despite the low rate of positive response in many cases, keep in mind that even cold calls should be thought out and prepared for, or you will fall into the 99.9 percent failure category. If you have acquired some kind of list related to your target audience, you still need to check on the potential and relevance of the contacts. This small amount of homework can save you time and the humility of continual rejection.

When making initial contact with a potential client, opening with "We offer this service or product that can improve your business" can be the fastest route to rejection. Personally, there is no quicker way to get me to hang up the phone or delete an e-mail than with this approach. Engage the contact by showing interest in what his or her company does, its core business, and what you contact's role may be in the organization. Let's face it, people like to talk about what they do more than listening to some stranger telling them what they are about or what their company has to offer. Leave that to the amateurs or those who have a canned spiel from some mass-marketing training course—and who have become immune to 99.9 percent rejection.

Personal Visits

Hands down, the best way to qualify a prospect is with a personal visit. This may require a few e-mail exchanges and phone calls, but to really get your finger on the pulse, there is nothing better than a face-to-face. See chapter 3 for tips on making the most of a face-to-face meeting with a potential customer.

Phone

I consider myself to be tech-savvy. I bought the first Android phone available (and four more since), am a prolific user of Office software—despite hating it—and stay current on the latest things going on with the Internet, website SEO, texting, social media, and other technical developments.

Having said all that, I still believe in using the telephone to make a more personal level of contact. At my current job, we frequently get e-mails and contact forms from our website. After filtering what is viable and what is a mismatch, I invariably pick up the phone to make initial contact. If you have the gift of the gab—and if you're in sales, you should—then pick up the damn phone. While purporting to be "current," there is nothing less personal to me than a generic e-mail or text message. Read what you have received, go and check out the company's website, and call the person with a modicum of knowledge about what they do. You will be surprised by how many people, even the younger generation, like to converse without typing with their thumbs or with a cryptic and often unclear e-mail reply. We are all wired differently, and it is so easy to misinterpret a message sent via e-mail. You cannot ask someone what they really need and what they are all about in a few lines of text. Short of a personal meeting, a phone call is the best way to learn what a person is looking for and what a company is about.

This, of course, applies to responses for information. Considering that we are focusing on capital and industrial products, there is no need to buy a contact list from some marketing entity and make hundreds or thousands of unsolicited phone calls. If you cannot qualify the contact as a real possibility through a bit of spade work, then don't bother making the call.

It's important to take notes when you call somebody or have any other type of contact. How you keep track of your interactions is a matter of personal choice. I use an old-fashioned notebook, noting the date and time of each contact, the name of the contact, and what was discussed. My own code marks in the left margin indicate if action is required, if a follow-up is needed, or if I need to do more work in order to get back to them with further information. I also place a number of stars to identify priority, just like kindergarten. (I did pick up something from going to school.) While I still enter electronic reminders on my PC and portable devices, I find going back through the written notes of previous correspondence is extremely helpful.

Another subtle yet frequently important aspect of a personal conversation is that you can get an idea of the type of person you are dealing with. People will not generally discuss their families, hobbies, or vacation plans in an e-mail. Do not underestimate the importance of small talk. People like talking about themselves, and once they have, they become more receptive to any information or offer that may ensue. If you are involved in sales, particularly of special, technical, or capital items, you will learn quickly the importance of rapport with your customers. If this is not in your DNA, then you may want to consider another profession, it's that important.

This may seem fundamental, but prior to making a call, especially the first one, take the time to write down some germane talking points. This will help you keep the conversation on track while coming to an early determination if there is a potential match.It is equally important to be able to have a normal conversation. If the discussion steers in the direction of a favorite vacation destination or your beloved pets or any other subject, go with the flow. If it becomes apparent during the early stages of discussion that there is not a fit, it is okay to politely bow out of further dialogue.

One of my current favorite customers is a company in Nova Scotia, Canada, that makes elaborate hydraulic systems for off-shore drilling rigs. My main contact is a woman named Monique who is married to the "brains" of the company. She is quite possibly the most pleasant person I have ever spoken to on the phone. While her company is not a huge customer in terms of sales, I always look forward to engaging in a conversation with her. From a business perspective, one may argue that this should require about five minutes, but every one of our conversations lasts more than twenty minutes. Some efficiency expert could make a case that this is a waste of time. All I know is that the company will never seek an alternate supplier, and I get the chance to be entertained with phone discussions with Monique four or five times a year.

As a matter of fact, with her sultry voice and her enthusiasm, we have hired her to do voice over on various videos and presentations.

E-mail (No Spam!)

In my mind, here are the best ways to communicate with potential clients, in order of effectiveness: (1) personal visits, (2) phone calls, (3) personal letters, (4) e-mail messages. Methods 3 and 4 are close to swapping spots as more and more of the business world favors expedience over substance. While e-mail is an easy and speedy mode of communication, less thought goes into the message. E-mail is a very efficient way to give a quick update of a delivery status or an FYI answer to a request. If it gets more complicated, your message should be better thought out and crafted prior to clicking *send*.

As a rule, a knee-jerk response is not a good idea. An old rule practiced and preached by most managers, especially to less-experienced employees, is to write your note or response to something and then put it in the top drawer of your desk—or in a draft folder—for at least a day. This is a particularly good plan if the response is negative or emotional. Nine times out of ten, you will either tear up your initial response or dramatically tone down the message. Dispute spawns more disputes, so it is always better to try to work toward a resolution and a positive step rather than reacting with pure emotion—even if the reaction is warranted.

Using e-mail properly can be a powerful marketing tool. Like every other tactic, it does require research and a focus on a specific audience, especially when dealing with engineered products. If you would like to send a message to a target group, take the time to filter the list so that it contains only those you want to target. Also, limit the message to a specific topic. If you sell engines and have a new development in the fuel-injection system, stay on point and talk about the new development, and avoid the broad-brush approach by trying to include (and cross market) the entire engine. This is a long-practiced piece of marketing advice, but in these days of instant messaging, and acknowledging that the attention span on an e-mail is less than one page scroll down, deliver your message at the very beginning. This age-old tactic harkens back to the "above the fold" tactic used by every editor since the beginning of newspapers. Few people will read an entire message once they know the basic content. This is especially true with an e-mail message, since clicking on delete is a far simpler option than reading three or four paragraphs of content. One other tactic with an e-mail rather than writing a tome in the e-mail body, is to write a note, memo or letter and attach it to the e-mail. Now, all you have to say in the e-mail - after the appropriate salutation – is to reference the attachment and what it is about. Then politely ask for there thoughts on your message.

If e-mail is your chosen method for contacting your audience, make it eye-catching enough to entice the reader to at least get through the message. This should include an attention grabber, such as a photograph, a quotation in bold, or another powerful component. The same holds true for other mass communication efforts, but is more applicable to the Attention Deficit Disorder audience of an e-mail blast. This is especially important when you're marketing industrial and capital goods. It is not difficult to focus on a specific group, but it does require effort to figure out who to include and who to forgo.

On a cautionary note, read receipts are generally met with disdain. If you are interested in the e-mail, you will respond in which case, a read receipt is supplanted with a return note. If you are not interested and want to delete it, why would acknowledge you read it knowing you are not going to respond?

Personally, I do my homework to develop my list of potentials and then create a database for one specific message to be delivered. This enables me to easily create a list of recipients and offers the benefit of updating or adding information about any potential customer as I receive feedback or they request information. In general, the market for a product—specifically industrial/custom or capital goods—can be narrowed down through experience and research. It should not be difficult to get your contact list down to one hundred or so if you put in the effort. Remember, these are not commodity products; they are truly suitable to a very specific list of targets. This group will appreciate it if some effort was put into finding them and offering a reason why there is a potential match. It also decreases the amount of follow-up effort required, since each addressee should be contacted at an appropriate time, whether with another e-mail or a phone call. Keep track of any and all correspondence.

Unsolicited Calls or Messages

Most of us receive unsolicited phone calls or e-mails from companies extolling their products. I must get five or ten of these every day. Of these calls, 99.9 percent of the time, service or product being touted has 0 percent relation to anything I or my company could use. It would have taken five minutes on Google or another search engine to figure this out before wasting time on an unfulfillable contact. In fact, this tactic can completely backfire. I am not alone in boycotting undesired solicitations with a note-to-self not to engage in business with a company that makes contact without prior notice. I'm referring only to specifically untargeted solicitations. There is, unfortunately, no control, because spam is here to stay, as is automated telemarketers working off lists provided by information-collection firms that call themselves marketing companies. These are easy to dismiss or delete if they are e-mail blasts. It is the ones who telephone you, mentioning the name of your company and perhaps even your name, to pitch something that neither you nor your company has any use for. This tactic requires the solicitor to read off a list purchased from some less-than-reputable marketing-information firm that is all about gathering phone numbers, e-mail addresses, and contact names, no matter how pertinent they may be. Mispronouncing your name is an obvious red flag.

While hardly ever a decent strategy for capital or technical goods, if you are going to cold contact groups, be sure to pick a particular product and develop a viable list of companies that at least have a chance of being interest. This pares down a mass-mail list or e-mail blast by tenfold or more, but increases the chance of a legitimate response and reduces the amount of space taken up in the spam landfill. Membership lists in pertinent nonprofessional societies or specific trade directories can help in some cases.

Written Letters

There is an ongoing and epidemic loss of the power of the written word. By written, I mean something that requires one to open a stamped envelope to reveal the contents addressed specifically to that person. In the world of selling, a personal touch is always better than a generic one. We have all received plenty of bulk mailings from charities, credit cards, retailers, and so on. I'm pretty sure I am not alone in depositing this type of mail directly in the recycling bin. However, you are far more likely to open a letter addressed to you and not to Occupant or Current Resident, with a real stamp. This is a bit of a stretch in the business world, but the point is to make your correspondence more likely to be opened and read. Further, the smaller your target audience, the better your chances for piquing interest. This, of course, requires doing more preparation before blasting out hundreds of letters. It's better still if you can handwrite a note on the letter to show that you took the time to actually learn about the recipient.

A targeted mail campaign is a completely different animal from a bulk mailing. Like everything else related to technical sales, it requires much up work up front. This can ensure you have narrowed the target audience to those most likely to fit. This method of marketing may be getting gray hair, but it can still be effective if you have an objective and focus on the message you send. The shotgun approach (more on that below) is extremely inefficient, especially if you do not screen the audience.

I don't use the written-letter tactic too often, but when I do, I generate a specific list or database of companies I intend to contact. It is essential to track their responses, or lack thereof, to further focus on the limited potential candidates. Going back to the phone-call rule, if you do get a response or have an indication of a good match, pick up the phone to learn the likelihood of a potential fit.

I admit that this technique is a bit archaic in today's world, but there still are prospects that are more likely to respond to this approach than more current methods. I still have contacts who do not use the Internet and ask for hard-copy product catalogs. Though this method is dying out, do not make the assumption that it is completely dead yet.

Shotgun Marketing

In the selling process for promoting capital, technical and industrial goods, the shotgun-marketing approach rarely comes into play, but bulk mailings or e-mail blasts are still methods appropriate for garnering new opportunities. It will be far more effective if you make your own list and not rely on some information-collection firm to generate one for you that you have to pay for. Pay for it with your own time and effort to ensure you compile an accurate target list. When employing this tactic, the target(s) should be screened for legitimacy. Even with due diligence to the potential prospects, understand that the success-to-failure ratio will still be relatively low, but at least you can increase your responses to way above the 99.9 percent failure ratio.

Websites

Your company website now provides the first impression for potential customers. They can make a decision, sometimes in seconds, as to whether they want to explore more about a potential fit. Complicated and overly wordy home pages can be a turnoff, since new prospects may not wish to invest the time to learn more about you. We live in the age of instant information, and if the information customers are looking can be found more easily elsewhere, they will go there if they find your website too difficult or frustrating to navigate. If you have any control or a say over what has become the front door to your company, remember to keep it simple with only items that can truly be considered "above the fold" included on the first page.

Navigation is an often overlooked aspect of a product-based website. There is no such thing as too few clicks of a mouse to obtain the information one is looking for. If your website requires more than three or four clicks to arrive at the desired information, your audience interest will be reduced significantly. There's that attention deficit again. This is complicated, because people are wired differently and some may have more patience than others. It is still best to assume that everyone visiting your site is impatient. When a person is searching for a product or company, the average time spent on a website is thought to be less than one minute, according to many web-marketing professionals. Create a reason for potential customers to stay longer by keeping things simple and easy to navigate.

The other key is to use your website as an entrée to customers and give them a reason to establish further contact. This works more like a résumé than a promotional tool. Since it is difficult to cover all selling points, make the visitors want more so that they will contact you directly. Whether a potential client is tech savvy or not, there is no replacement for direct conversation.

One of my favorite comments when I receive a phone call is, "I'm on your website, and I'm looking for more information about a product I may be interested in." Bingo! I've just established personal contact with a potential customer. If this same person had accessed the website and not found anything that piqued his interest, he would not have called.

While I am not a professional web developer, I am certain I represent the majority of people who use the Internet to do product research. When I access a website and I cannot figure out where to go, I leave. If it is not apparent where I can find what I need, I leave. If it is not easy to find a way to contact the company with a question, I leave. And, being picky, if the site is not well presented or is obviously behind the times, I am inclined to leave, but may stick around if I have a quick and easy point of contact. Keep it simple and do not put too much information on the site that then negatively affects navigation.

Make the site easy to navigate, which probably involves someone else evaluating this feature. Make it easy to communicate with your company, whether by e-mail, phone, chat room, or a contact form. It is equally important to respond to requests within a reasonable time frame; twenty-four hours is a good benchmark. In today's world, twenty-four hours may as well be a week or more. The key here is to respond. You may not have a specific answer, but at least acknowledge receipt of the request and a reason why you need time to respond. Personally, I try to follow up with a phone call as I believe this is more personal. If voice mail or tedious phone menus makes this difficult, than at least a message by voice or e-mail will let the person know you received the inquiry and are working on an answer.

From a user's—not a developer's—aspect, it's important to keep the site fresh and up-to-date. But don't change everything unless there is a compelling reason. I do most of the cooking and grocery shopping in our house. We are all creatures of habit, and when I walk into my usual grocery story and everything has moved, it makes it more time consuming to find what I want. I want to go to a location, store, website, or other place of commerce, find exactly what I want, and then leave. I am not a shopper, nor are the vast majority of the Internet users, particularly those looking at specialty products. Altering the location of information on a website is akin to rearranging the products in a grocery store.

Website design, promotion, content, and appearance will, of course, vary with specific goals. For capital and industrial products that mainly require technical discussions, the better call to action for a website is to drive the potential client to establish contact directly, since all variables cannot be reasonably covered in a few web pages. The site is for branding rather than selling a product or for e-commerce.

Leaving the importance of your website analytics to those who know what this means, there are tools available to track the traffic to your website that do not require a PhD to figure out. Your webmaster or whomever hosts and maintains your website can do this and issue monthly reports. From these you can see what direction traffic is trending to your site, what content visitors are looking for, and even where your site is positioned on popular search engines. This can tell you if you want to consider employing a professional search engine optimization (SEO) company to improve your rankings. It really does work. You learn who has been on your site, how much time they spent, and what they looked at. This also enables you to target those who are legitimate candidates for follow up, given the amount and quality of time they have spent on your site. Reread the e-mail or written-letter section to learn the best way to follow up a decent lead. Analytic sites such as Google are easy to set-up and navigate even if you are not a computer whiz-bang. This allows you to monitor your web traffic from the comfort of your own desk or laptop or tablet or smart phone. The bottom line is the readily available technology to keep track of visitors to your web site.

My company recently embarked on a new website design, even though it's been only five years since a total overhaul. The technology and ability to track web traffic has changed immensely in the past five years and will probably continue to do so for the foreseeable future. Our web designer, which also serves as our principal advertising and marketing firm, offered some new website development software based on the latest technology to carry out the task. While we were in agreement not to change the theme or content too much, the objective was to update the code and freshen the appearance. There is a new a code capable of recognizing the device on which the site is being viewed, including HD flat-screen TVs, laptops, tablets, and smart phones. The pages automatically adjust to accommodate the size of the screen being used. Previously, many websites had a mobile version, usually with the same URL but preceded by "m.domainname.com." These mobile sites had restricted access in the interests of accommodating a smaller screen. The new software enables any visitor to a website to have full access without compromising content. It was a bit more expensive to go this way, but you cannot stop technology. I am sure the next time we go through a website overhaul, other newer software and techniques will be available, making our current site seem obsolete. If I have learned anything about technology, especially related to the Internet and websites, it is to remain current, despite the speed of change.

I am writing this on a computer with a 500 gigabyte hard drive and more RAM than all the Dodge truck dealers combined. I hark back to my first PC experience on a Radio Shack TRS-80, with keyboard buttons the size of ice cubes, a monochrome screen, and a thousand times less memory than my smart phone. I do not miss the early 1980s. Times change, and you should go along with them or be lost in the slipstream.

Web Tools: Blogs and Social Media Outlets

Back in the good old days, it was stylish and current to have a website, but it was not a necessity. That is no longer the case. A company's website serves as its front door. It is the main source for a first impression for new or potential customers. Appearance, navigability, and remaining current are imperatives for any organization's website. It is important to drive traffic to your site, which requires the use of the latest techniques, including constant change and monitoring, analytics, and using a dedicated SEO service to improve ranking positions on popular search engines.

New methods for website visibility and Internet presence include blogs and tying into social media. There are good ways and bad ways to use these tools. Regardless, the most important aspect is to monitor and maintain your content. If you have a Facebook page for your company, you now have an open book and can be susceptible to negative feedback or outright fallacies. If you choose to use social media to promote your company, it must be monitored or comments from visitors must be approved. It is equally important to maintain a consistent level of updates and not let things take on a life of their own or gather mold. Any company blog or social-media account that has little to no activity will be stale and boring, sending negative vibes to anyone viewing your posts. If you or someone assigned to manage this process is unable to remain current, then you are better off not even participating.

Increase Your Web Presence

For engineered products and capital goods, the common sites such as Facebook and Twitter present little opportunity for promotion and reaching a target audience. The main and perhaps only purpose of using these sites is to increase your web presence and branding your company. The more posts made around the web, particularly using product names and keywords, the more highly ranked your website becomes on search engines. Thus, the social-media sites serve as a means to boost your SEO. Bear in mind that if the posts about your company or products to such sites are not routinely updated with new content, the less they will contribute to any SEO program. Unless there are internal resources within your company to handle SEO activity, it is paramount to find a good and ethical SEO company to assist with keeping your company's website near the top of rankings on search tools such as Google. This is an ongoing and ever-changing process, and I do not proclaim to know how it works. But I do know that my company's keywords consistently rank on the first page of major search engines. Considering a company's website is the first impression for any potential or existing client, it is crucial that the site is easily accessed, and accessibility occurs largely via search engines.

LinkedIn and YouTube

LinkedIn is the most prominent social media site that can be useful for company marketing. It is geared toward business management and has become an increasingly effective and popular tool for business professionals. The most common use of LinkedIn is as a networking tool to find services or talent that fill a company's or individual's need. It also works in much the same way as other social-media outlets to improve your web presence for SEO purposes. It's easy to set up a company account on LinkedIn, but bear in mind, the same rules apply about monitoring and updating on a consistent basis.

Having a company YouTube account with videos is one of the most effective ways of improving a company's website presence in search engines. I do not know how this works exactly, but I have been in continuous contact with my current company's SEO firm, and they persistently ask for videos to post to YouTube. Apparently, Google likes videos.

Other ways to get your website noticed is to have numerous hyperlinks from other sites. This could be paid for on trade-publication sites, on industrial information sites such as ThomasNet, from partner companies (suppliers and customers), or via news releases sent to a variety of media outlets. Ideally, these links should point to the page on your website that is specific to the topic presented. Just arranging links to a home page is not nearly as effective as pointing to a specific product or service within the site.

Your marketing program can be improved by the use of avenues outside your website, such as social media. In order for this tactic to be most successful, put sufficient time into maintenance and keeping information fresh. Also, monitor the analytics to these sites to see the quantity and types of hits you are getting. Don't be afraid to issue releases related to your participation in these sites, in addition to the now common icons embedded in your company's website.

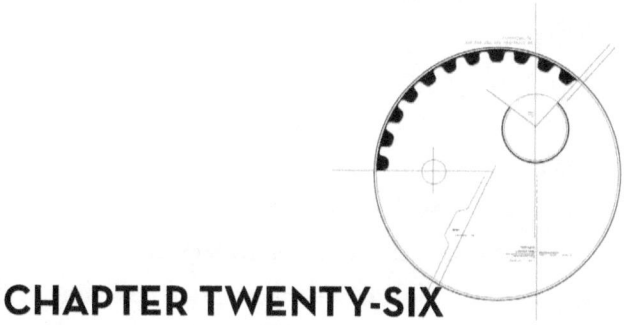

CHAPTER TWENTY-SIX

Other Product Promotion Techniques

By now you should know that selling unique, custom-built capital equipment is totally different from commodity sales. It is not possible to sell a product that doesn't exist or that not has already been defined by the desired process or task. So, to promote what you offer is to promote your company's capabilities and yourself. Capabilities are largely based on your company's reputation and the history of what it has accomplished. This can get tricky, because it may not be possible to mention previous or current clients' names or projects you have engaged in, for proprietary reasons. It may seem like an inconsequential detail when dealing with new customers, particularly in an intriguing application, but getting approval to use the client's name and discuss the specific application for promotional purposes is best done as part of the initial process.

Getting Permission to Use Real Clients

In many cases, you may be dealing with a large company or one that has regulations to deal with. This is intrinsically bureaucratic and makes it time consuming, so it may not be worth the effort to gain approval for

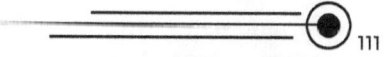

using information related to the application or the company using your products. There is no need to force an entity to agree for you to use its name or how your products are applied, as it may create some friction. But it is far smoother to do so prior to actually delivering the product. You can present a success story without mentioning the client unless they own the rights to the design, but it far better to use the name of your customer.

If you're unsuccessful in gaining support for marketing your products prior to a "sexy" sale, make the promotion appealing to the customer. The term *free advertising* can be used. However, it is more complicated than just convincing your customer to allow you to use their name and reference the specific use of your product. While you may deal in depth with project people and ultimately purchasing personnel, it can be valuable to learn about the entire food chain, including the marketing department. They have nothing to do with procurement, but may be intrigued about promotional opportunities. Once again, homework and knowing as much as possible about the organization and the process of each transaction is invaluable.

My company recently sold hydraulic valves to Space Exploration Technologies Corp., aka SpaceX, to be used to elevate their privately funded rockets into a launch position. While our product was a small part of the entire project, it is still noteworthy and has enough sex appeal to use as a promotional tool. We gained approval to use the name and details of how our products were used prior to the final sale. While this was an insubstantial part of our bottom line, it certainly piqued interest in other potential customers. SpaceX intends to launch the most powerful rocket ever built in late 2015, and just saying we played a role makes an impressive statement of our company accomplishments.

Media

Conventional media, meaning print ads or trade shows, are dinosaurs in my opinion, unless you have a commodity product. Most technical or capital products do not qualify as viable candidates for print ads. The only redeeming quality for companies involved with custom/

technical or capital products is company awareness or branding. The World Wide Web has ensured this will not change. Efforts in digital ads, industry-specific websites, or organizations are time and money better spent.

No disrespect to the print media, but fewer and fewer professionals use trade publications as a source for information. Search engines can provide anything at the click of a mouse, or even a voice command if you've gone there. There still is a place, perhaps in the … ahem … bathroom for printed magazines, but essentially, the world has gone digital and your promotions should take that into account. Besides, smart phones or tablets work in the bathroom!

While slightly behind print media, trade shows are also slowly lessening in significance. Many larger corporations still want to make a splash at McCormick Place in Chicago or the Messe in Düsseldorf, Germany, but the rewards have diminished. As a marketing veteran, I have always found it difficult to justify the expense of participating in one of these major shows. *Intangibility* was my only explanation, and that reason is also diminishing as people turn more and more to the web to do research and gather information for a product. Since a company can make a splash with Internet marketing and an informative and efficient website, the intangibility factor has decreased and continues to trend in that direction.

Bottom line: if you decide on a non-digital promotion method, make sure you have an objective and don't have high expectations. There are no tangible analytics for print media or trade shows. If your goal is branding or corporate presence, then it may be justified. If the intention is to sell specially built or capital products, then think of another way to do so. Becoming one of the leaders in the field at what you produce is a solid objective, as it builds confidence in potential clients. However, you cannot expect to sell using conventional media or trade outlets.

Trade Conferences

Trade conferences are another non-digital promotional technique. Conferences are the bailiwick of the curious and technical, but not of procurement or financial, so keep that in mind. However, a conference can vault a certain level of credibility, provided you can present something that most (if not all) of the audience hasn't heard before. This is still a good platform to offer new technology or even a public service announcement. This is a long-practiced piece of marketing advice, but in these days of instant messaging, and acknowledging that the attention span on an e-mail is less than a few seconds according to studies, so make your point at the beginning of your message.

> Not long ago, I gave a presentation at a conference on the safety of equipment used in compressing and delivering pure oxygen. As you may know, this application is what caused the fire and tragic death of three astronauts in the infant stages of the Apollo program. Neither physics nor chemistry has changed, and dealing with pure oxygen at high pressures can be inherently risky. This risk is minimized if the proper precautions are taken in terms of cleanliness, and proper training is adhered to. I was frankly amazed at the number of people in the audience who had limited knowledge about the dangers of environments saturated in pure oxygen, especially at elevated pressures. While our company spells this out in detail, replete with warnings and cautions, users still use compressed oxygen systems in a very irresponsible way.

Conferences and other events, including sales meeting, offer the unique opportunity of reaching a large audience in a personal matter. The only thing better is a one-on-one meeting, but that requires relationship building and a mutual benefit. Presentations about a specific topic given to a specific audience that signed up to participate can help reach a broad range of potential clients without as much homework. More imaginative things such as hosting an open house at your facility with a tour, a lunch and then a brief presentation to the attendees is not a novel idea, but is rarely done.I'm not fond of this phrase, but think outside the box to keep existing customers up to speed and also, perhaps, get the attention of new potentials.

CHAPTER TWENTY-SEVEN

Public Speaking

Whether presenting to a small group or speaking to an auditorium of people at a conference, carrying yourself with confidence is as important as the content of the message you deliver. The best way to keep an audience engaged is to know your subject matter cold, which can be accomplished only by preparation and practice. There is no worse situation than winging it, especially on a topic you may not be comfortable with. Know your topic, be concise and precise, and rehearse the content—including language, tone of voice, and body language. There is no faster way to lose an audience than by being hesitant or showing a lack of confidence. (Watch a YouTube clip of Steve Jobs introducing a product or addressing shareholders. I have seen no one better with command, control, conviction, and confidence.) Most initial nervousness about addressing a crowd can be overcome by knowing your material inside and out—and by practicing your delivery.

Practice Makes Perfect

There is not a better way to appear confident and knowledgeable about your subject matter than preparing and practicing until you know the material by heart. Yes, homework again. Be sure to engage the audience with eye contact and let your personality come through. Be aware of the audience's reaction and make adjustments if you are losing the crowd. There is nothing wrong with making a long pause, taking a deep breath, and visually checking the audience's mood. You can make a quick content adjustment if necessary. Perhaps engage the audience with a story or a question about what they are looking for. It's not a weakness. Involving your audience can be the best way to earn back or retain its interest.

Get Their Attention Quickly

Get your audience's attention from the get-go. The most common way of doing this is by injecting an interesting personal experience or an amusing story into your opening remarks. This can be most effective if you know your audience and can customize your opening comments to them. You must be careful not to step over the edge with satire or jokes. In other words, leave your Rodney Dangerfield at the door.

Once the audience is relaxed and receptive, it will be easier to get your message across—provided you have material people want to hear and it is presented with professionalism. As importantly, cater your presentation to the audience. Even if you feel it is overly simplified, you need to prepare and deliver to the lowest common denominator. If you cannot find out what that level is in advance, then assume it to be lower rather than higher. If you read the situation differently once you're there, then adjust accordingly. It is paramount to be the smartest person in the room on the topic(s) you are presenting while remaining humble and understanding. This is confidence and humility; a great combination.

Dealing with Hecklers

You do not have to be a politician to be aware that there are critics or even hecklers in every audience. The two ways to deal with this are to ignore or to respond, ignoring being the first course of action. Responding requires thinking on your feet and deflecting the remarks with gentle humor or a strong demonstration of your knowledge of the subject matter. It is not inappropriate to engage hecklers by acknowledging their knowledge (or lack thereof) of the topic. Hecklers usually have big egos and know-it-all attitudes, and they like to engage in negative discourse. The last and probably worst option is to express anger, as you are likely to alienate your audience. But on rare occasions, an offensive comment should be dealt with assertively, though as tastefully as possible, with a calm voice and not confrontational.

The Benefit of Extensive Preparation

Back in 1995, I was speaking at a conference in Singapore regarding plastic-processing equipment, my profession at the time. I was fortunate to have a knowledgeable PhD from the United Kingdom go before me. He put the audience to sleep with boring statistics, reading off a script and showing no energy or personality. Since this was my first large international conference presentation, I had created a PowerPoint presentationwith animations and embedded video (high tech at the time). I had practiced the material over and over and required no script, much like an actor knowing his lines. Based on the prior speaker, I decided to be more enthusiastic and demonstrative. I knew these things were important, but so much of presenting is about your personality, which you cannot fake. I was able to walk around the stage confidently, sans notes, emphasizing points when necessary, and received a large ovation when I was done. A satisfying feeling indeed, and all because I cared how I would be perceived and had prepared extensively.

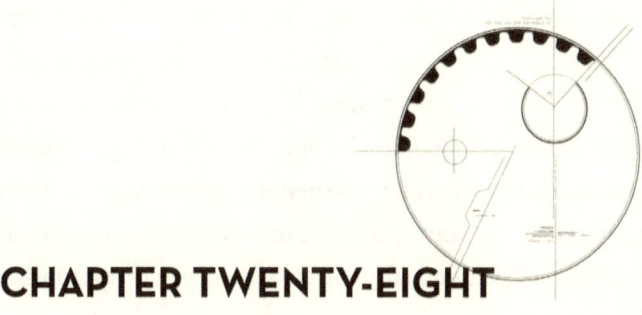

CHAPTER TWENTY-EIGHT

Closing Thoughts

Selling Has Changed in the Last Thirty Years

I cannot speak to selling strategies before the late eighties, when I started my career. But in my opinion, the entire process of selling, marketing, and doing business has undergone a sea change since that time. I remember my first e-mail address, and it was the equivalent of getting a phone book for the first time. Both made you feel more relevant and up to speed with current times. Now that I have had roughly fifteen different e-mail accounts, Skype, and various social media accesses, it is clear to anyone who has not just crawled out from under a rock that the world has changed.

I am experienced enough to remember when the three-martini lunch transformed into a one-beer session, to the current day when offering to take a customer to lunch or dinner is against company policy. This may be a challenge to old-school salespeople, particularly in certain industries, but it has morphed the process of establishing a relationship without getting your prospect tipsy first. This does not in any way diminish the importance of establishing a relationship. The difference is that it is done with responsiveness, understanding, and interest in the issue at hand.

Lunch has mostly been replaced with cordiality and prompt reaction to the needs of whomever you deal with. Don't me wrong if lunch or a drink after work is on the table, then by all means use it.

Part of this new process is to be accurate with any response or correspondence. Perhaps it's me, but when I get e-mails that are not grammatically correct, with spelling errors and all in lower-case letters, I judge. It may be unwarranted, but it is a first impression. It is not hard to structure a grammatically correct sentence with appropriate punctuation. At the very least, there is no excuse not to converse accurately. First impressions matter.

Written or verbal communication is also relative to the audience. Be sure to factor that in when corresponding. Whether it is an old-school mentality or a different culture, adjust the message to suit. It is not difficult to check into the preferred nature of the message, depending on who is being addressed.

I Know I've Said This Before, But...

When selling to any industry or culture, never start with a negative thought, and remember to do your homework.

Nuff said.

ABOUT THE AUTHOR

Mike Hotchkiss is a mechanical engineer by degree who has spent the bulk of his professional life marketing and selling capital machinery and engineered products designed for specific applications. While living in Singapore for five years, he spent much of his time traveling the world for various projects, gaining valuable insight into different business cultures and selling techniques.

Currently, he is mostly grounded and running the sales and marketing function at Interface Devices, Inc., founded by his father, Thomas Hotchkiss.

Mike lives contentedly in the New Haven, Connecticut, area with his wife, Sue, and three adopted rescue dogs.

INDEX

1. Learn before Engaging..2
2. Here's a True Story 3
3. Every Sale Is Unique 3
4. Research Your Potential Customer............................5
5. Know the Company's DNA.......................................6
6. Cultural Considerations...7
7. One Thing You Shouldn't Do 7
8. What Is the Customer's Hierarchy?..........................8
9. At Trade Shows No Yes or No Questions.................8
10. No "How Can I Help You?" 9
11. A Case of My Company Being the Customer 10
12. A Case in Point..10
13. Selling Dos and Don'ts Do Ask Questions.............11
14. Do Let the Customer Be in Charge 11
15. Do Take Time for a Friendly Chat..........................11
16. Don't Go Negative...12
17. Don't Talk about Controversial Topics...................12
18. Don't Excuse Bad Behavior.....................................12
19. Setting an Agenda..14
20. "I'll Get Back to You on That".................................15
21. Other Sources of Information 16
22. First Impressions Are Important 16
23. Find Out the Purpose of the Meeting.....................20
24. Demonstrate Sincere Interest 21
25. Preparation and Patience Paid Off 21

26.	It's Like a First Date	23
27.	Get to Know the Supporting Cast	24
28.	Ask to Meet the Person Who Signs the Purchase Order	24
29.	Know the Company's Hierarchy	25
30.	Keep Track of Change	26
31.	Another True Story: I Never Saw It Coming	26
32.	Fill the Hole	28
33.	Find Out What the Customer Needs	30
34.	Don't Promise Something You Can't Deliver	31
35.	Keep Everyone in Your Company in the Loop	31
36.	A Painful True Story	31
37.	Always Reply Promptly	33
38.	Leaving E-mail Messages	34
39.	Tweaking the Proposal	36
40.	It's Their Job to Get the Best Deal	37
41.	"I'll Get Back to You on That"	38
42.	Keep Your Cool	38
43.	You Never Know How a Deal Will Close	39
44.	Rely on Your Research … and Your Gut	40
45.	Acknowledge the Customer's Request	41
46.	Service after the Sale	42
47.	Get Information from up and down the Company Ladder	43
48.	Be Honest about Your Capabilities	44
49.	Larger Orders Take More Time	45
50.	Even Seasoned Salespeople Occasionally Sweat	45
51.	When You Have to Say No	47
52.	When There's Disrespect	48
53.	Find a Middle Ground	49
54.	Your Challenge: Breaking Old Buying Patterns	51
55.	Be Honest with Your Company Contacts	52
56.	A True Story about Good Customer Relations	53
57.	Know What Makes Your Customer Tick	56

58.	Don't Promise What You Can't Deliver	56
59.	Follow Up after the Meeting	56
60.	Stay in Touch	57
61.	Establish Rapport	58
62.	Follow Up to Their Requests	59
63.	Maintain Post-order Contact	59
64.	No News Is Not Necessarily Good News	60
65.	Know What Every Tentacle Is Doing	63
66.	If You're Pushed to Do More	63
67.	Stay on Top of the Process and Progress	64
68.	Keep on Top of Post-order Progress	65
69.	Stick to Your Core Competency	66
70.	Be Punctual	66
71.	Take Control If There's a Problem after Delivery	67
72.	Collect the Facts	68
73.	Don't Encourage Unfounded Opinions	69
74.	Make Sure the Right People Are Problem Solving	69
75.	A Sample Chain of Miscommunication	72
76.	Take Ownership of the Problem	73
77.	Don't Make Comparisons with Your Competition	75
78.	Know What the Competition Is Offering	76
79.	Offer an Extended Warranty	77
80.	Sell the Benefits of Your Own Product	78
81.	Real-Life Lessons	79
82.	Clients Can Change Their Minds	81
83.	Negotiate Order-Entry Issues Honestly	82
84.	When New Requests Are Put on the Table	83
85.	Sometimes It's an Internal Issue	83
86.	I Agree, But …	84
87.	Again, Take Ownership	85
88.	Inside Impediments to the Sales Process	86
89.	A Hard Lesson Learned	87

90. Motivating an International Sales Team.................................88
91. Keep Everyone in the Loop.......................................89
92. Agents...90
93. Distributors 91
94. Motivate Your Outside Agents 92
95. Make Them Look Good 93
96. Information Gathering Is Still the Key to the Sale 93
97. Make Sure They Understand Your Product Inside and Out 94
98. Preparing Your Mailing List 95
99. Don't Force a Fit 96
100. Cold-Calling..96
101. Personal Visits...97
102. Phone...97
103. E-mail (No Spam!) 99
104. Unsolicited Calls or Messages 102
105. Written Letters 103
106. Shotgun Marketing.. 104
107. Websites... 104
108. Web Tools: Blogs and Social Media Outlets.................... 108
109. Increase Your Web Presence................................... 109
110. LinkedIn and YouTube 109
111. Getting Permission to Use Real Clients 111
112. Media 112
113. Trade Conferences 114
114. Practice Makes Perfect 117
115. Get Their Attention Quickly...................................117
116. Dealing with Hecklers 118
117. The Benefit of Extensive Preparation..........................118
118. I Know I've Said This Before, But … 120

www.ingramcontent.com/pod-product-compliance
Lightning Source LLC
Chambersburg PA
CBHW021956170526
45157CB00003B/1019